Engaging English Learners Through Access to Standards

To
Scott and Nora
—S. F.

To
My rock and inspiration, Vinh
—S. J. V.

And to our many students and families
from around the world
who are the reason for our work.

Engaging English Learners Through Access to Standards

A Team-Based Approach to Schoolwide Student Achievement

Shelley Fairbairn | Stephaney Jones-Vo

Foreword by Jeff Zwiers

CORWIN
A SAGE Company

A SAGE Company

FOR INFORMATION:

Corwin

A SAGE Company

2455 Teller Road

Thousand Oaks, California 91320

(800) 233-9936

www.corwin.com

SAGE Publications Ltd.

1 Oliver's Yard

55 City Road

London EC1Y 1SP

United Kingdom

SAGE Publications India Pvt. Ltd.

B 1/I 1 Mohan Cooperative Industrial Area

Mathura Road, New Delhi 110 044

India

SAGE Publications Asia-Pacific Pte. Ltd.

3 Church Street

#10-04 Samsung Hub

Singapore 049483

Program Director: Dan Alpert

Senior Associate Editor: Kimberly Greenberg

Editorial Assistant: Cesar Reyes

Production Editor: Veronica Stapleton Hooper

Copy Editor: Cate Huisman

Typesetter: C&M Digitals (P) Ltd.

Proofreader: Annie Lubinsky

Indexer: Jeanne R. Busemeyer

Cover Designer: Anupama Krishnan

Marketing Manager: Stephanie Trkay

Printed in the United States of America

ISBN 978-1-4833-1988-9

This book is printed on acid-free paper.

SFI Certified Sourcing
www.sfiprogram.org
SFI-00453

15 16 17 18 19 10 9 8 7 6 5 4 3 2 1

Contents

Foreword

In our current journey as educators to serve all students as best as we can, we are at an exciting and challenging point of convergence. Many states have accepted and created new standards for college and career readiness. These standards have been accompanied by calls for major shifts in instruction and assessment, especially for meeting the needs of English learners and others who will struggle with the new cognitive and linguistic demands. A heightened focus on rigor and language development across disciplines also converges here. And a deeper emphasis on valid evidence, not just test score numbers, has joined the flow. The ever-increasing numbers of English learners, the ongoing challenge of teacher turnover, and the lack of resources in high-need schools are at this point of convergence, too.

As the authors of *Engaging English Learners Through Access to Standards: A Team-Based Approach to Schoolwide Student Achievement* argue, we must implement a differentiated approach; emphasize the learning of content, thinking, and academic language; and do so in research-based and creative ways. How? With a team-based approach that is focused on a clear and shared vision, which is much easier said than done in diverse school settings.

The many challenges of educating English learners cannot be overcome in isolation; educators must work together, and very efficiently, given the enormous time demands. Most administrators and teachers, for example, have overflowing schedules filled by the many needs of students, assessment, and lesson planning and delivery. The ENGAGE model is a powerful way to address this mix of challenges. The model first helps a team to establish a shared vision for English learners and consider how instruction and assessment can serve these students rather than alienate them. Then it guides the team in maximizing the talents and expertise within its ranks. Next, the model explains the strategic gathering and use of data on English learners in various areas of academic growth within a defined setting. In the fourth phase, it helps educators design assessments and grading practices that accurately address English learners' current levels of language use, skill, and content understanding. Finally, the authors discuss integrating language to support content development and looking at results to inform next steps, offering practical approaches to these tasks.

Throughout the book are many helpful charts that clarify the responsibilities team members can assume at each stage to ensure success. Our students, especially those who struggle the most, deserve a powerful system with skilled team members who know how to work together to meet their needs. The ENGAGE model described in these pages offers a helpful set of tools, grounded in the latest research, for growing an effective team that maximizes its potential to meet the varied needs of English learners.

Jeff Zwiers
Senior Researcher, Stanford University Graduate School of Education

Preface

THE NEED FOR THIS BOOK

Standards of teaching and learning have taken center stage across the nation, with the expectation that *all* students will achieve at high levels. Against this backdrop, the fastest-growing population under 18 in the United States (Mather, 2009) is often left behind: English learners. In spite of the seminal Supreme Court decision, *Lau v. Nichols* (1974), which requires explicit attention to the linguistic needs of ELs in mainstream classrooms and was passed down over 40 years ago, the specific linguistic needs of English learners go largely unmet in many districts/schools.

Given the current vast shortage of ESL teachers and the ongoing failure to prepare mainstream classroom teachers to teach the ELs in their class-rooms, it is overwhelmingly evident that a clear, step-by-step guide is needed to address the needs of English learners. These ELs increasingly represent a significant percentage of student enrollment in many districts/schools.

This book was born of the desire to assist and support districts/schools in systemically undertaking the change needed to focus on the academic achievement of ELs. The model described within addresses the current inequitable state of affairs by advocating for the comprehensive inclusion of ELs in classroom practice by providing them access to the standards-based curriculum, rooted in an orientation of informed empathy and understanding of the range of EL background characteristics that drive instructional needs.

The authors have developed a team-based approach to schoolwide student achievement with a focus on ELs. This book details the steps needed to effect positive change in K–12 schools to provide ELs access to a standards-based curriculum. It addresses such topics as

- Mobilizing district/school teams to cultivate a collective will and vision to serve ELs
- Establishing buy-in from all educators and stakeholders that will motivate sustained effort

- Inspecting data through an "EL Lens" to ascertain and ensure its utility and meaning for ELs
- Defining roles of each district/school administrator, teacher, and stakeholder in supporting EL success
- Implementing linguistically differentiated standards-based instruction and assessment in K–12 classrooms, based on student data
- Adopting and implementing standards-based differentiated grading for ELs

Given projections for continuing growth of the EL population in US schools, and given the fact that many school districts already report majority EL enrollment, it is time to acknowledge the importance of ELs as young future leaders who have an urgent need to receive a rigorous education that will result in college and career readiness. The dividends of providing this preparation are obvious in terms of benefits to individuals, families, communities, and economies. Not providing such rigorous education represents an unacceptable and embarrassing waste of human potential. While the appropriate education of ELs in the United States is a challenging task due to the need to simultaneously develop both English language proficiency and content knowledge, skills, and abilities, the potential rewards to students, families, and communities are great and nonnegotiable.

THE ORGANIZATION OF THIS BOOK

In **Chapter 1**, the overview of the **ENGAGE** model outlines the components for engaging ELs by providing access to standards-based achievement using a district/school team-based approach:

- Establish a shared vision grounded in deep understanding of ELs.
- Name and capitalize upon relevant expertise within collaborative teams.
- Gather and analyze EL-specific data.
- Align standards-based assessments and grading with ELs' current levels of linguistic and content development.
- Ground standards-based instruction in content *and* language development.
- Examine results to inform and drive next steps.

Detailing the need for change in meeting the needs of ELs, **Chapter 1** grounds districts/schools in shifting demographics and describes current issues in schools that fail to meet EL needs. Suffering from overrepresentation in special education and a disproportionately high dropout rate, ELs clearly are in need of advocacy, instruction, and support. Chapter 1 motivates districts/schools to adopt the team-based approach described by the ENGAGE model to address these issues both systemically and systematically, based on a shared vision for engaging and serving ELs.

Chapter 2 supports district/school leaders and teams by offering guidance in how to *Establish a shared vision for serving ELs* grounded in an understanding of the realities of these students. This essential foundational step describes the importance of cultivating a district/school collective will to support ELs and provides a compass to guide future actions in team-based work to support ELs at the district/school level.

Chapter 3 expands on the ENGAGE model by fleshing out what it means to *Name and capitalize upon relevant expertise within collaborative teams.* This step in the process is essential for illuminating internal resources, allowing stakeholders in the EL teaching/learning process to call upon each other for meaningful support in their work to facilitate EL academic achievement. Useful templates are shared in this chapter and throughout the book for teams to refer to and utilize during implementation of the ENGAGE model. In addition, ideas for establishing mechanisms for communication and collaboration, sharing expertise, and celebrating successes are detailed.

Chapter 4 describes how to *Gather and analyze EL-specific data.* While many team members will be familiar with traditional data that are often applied to ELs, this chapter describes the inappropriate and ill-advised nature of relying on data that are generated by assessments not designed for ELs and that do not take into account their background characteristics. The notion of interpreting EL data through an EL Lens is offered as a tool to enhance understanding of what ELs know and can do, both in English and in the content areas. Collection of additional relevant EL data is encouraged and described. This chapter lays out the process for convening collaborative teams and for increasing district/school capacity to use data to drive EL instruction and assessment. The specific roles and responsibilities of three levels of districtwide/schoolwide personnel (administrators, teachers, and other stakeholders) are described in detail in this chapter and the next two.

Chapter 5 focuses on an essential practice for teachers of ELs: how to *Align standards-based assessments and grading with ELs' current levels of linguistic and content development.* The authors describe and detail this alignment process through clear analysis of both English language development/proficiency levels and content abilities. Teachers are guided in the process of creating assessments that are appropriate for ELs in terms of language and content demands. Finally, the authors advocate for a differentiated standards-based grading process that acknowledges EL learning in keeping with their linguistic and content instructional levels.

Chapter 6 describes the next component: how to **G**round *standards-based instruction in content* and *language development.* EL-appropriate curriculum design and instructional materials are discussed, along with research-based practices found to support ELs and linguistically differentiated teaching strategies for use in the classroom on a daily basis. The chapter offers a variety of practical suggestions and includes resources for district/school teams to use when implementing instruction that attends to both language and content development.

Examine results to inform and drive next steps is the final component of the ENGAGE model. **Chapter 7** underscores the cyclical and spiraling nature of examining and interpreting data, adjusting practice, and redoubling efforts to achieve improved results. In addition, a helpful resource designed to assist teams in evaluating their work is provided in template form.

We hope that, through adopting and implementing the ENGAGE model, districts/schools will be empowered to engage ELs in equitable learning opportunities by providing access to standards through

- Differentiating linguistic and curricular expectations based on accurately interpreted data
- Affording ELs parity of access to the curriculum through differentiated instruction
- Implementing grading policies that provide accurate and meaningful information for ELs and their families
- And most important, supporting ELs in demonstrating increased achievement grounded in standards

Publisher's Acknowledgments

Corwin gratefully acknowledges the contributions of the following reviewers:

Cynthia Church
Principal
G. Stanley Hall Elementary School
Glendale Heights, IL

David G. Daniels
Principal
Susquehanna Valley Senior High
  School
Conklin, NY

Delsia Malone
Principal
W. E. Striplin Elementary School
Gadsden, AL

Sharon Padget
ESL Teacher
Ottumwa High School
Ottumwa, Iowa

Diane Senk
ELL Teacher
Sheboygan Area School District
Sheboygan, WI

About the Authors

Shelley Fairbairn, PhD, is a veteran ESL/EFL teacher and an associate professor in the Drake University School of Education in Des Moines, Iowa. Her teaching foci include preparing preservice teachers to design effective lesson plans and assessments for K–12 students and empowering both pre- and in-service teachers to meet the needs of English learners through linguistically and culturally responsive practice. Prior to joining the Drake University School of Education faculty, Dr. Fairbairn concurrently taught ESL courses for the Drake University International Center and served as a K–12 ESL teacher in two Des Moines area school districts.

Dr. Fairbairn's international experience includes three years of teaching English as a foreign language in Jakarta, Indonesia, and one year of teaching ESL and ESL certificate courses at the Regional Language Centre in Singapore. More recently, she has conducted teacher professional development sessions and workshops in China, Canada, and across the United States, often with Stephaney Jones-Vo, her coauthor of *Differentiating Instruction and Assessment for English Language Learners: A Guide for K–12 Teachers* (Caslon Publishing). Her additional scholarly work focuses primarily on effective assessment and instructional practices for ELs.

Stephaney Jones-Vo, MA, graduated from Iowa State University specializing in TESL (Linguistics). She has provided professional development on K–12 and adult ESL and diversity topics for over two decades for numerous school districts across the United States and around the world. She has designed and delivered ESL curricula for a variety of medical programs; developed and taught job-specific ESL classes for manufacturing and hospitality industries; and consulted with and presented at universities, medical schools, and businesses on engaging English learners and enhancing cultural competence. She also dedicated 10 years to a successful teaching career in a K–12 ESL program that she founded.

Personal involvement in the refugee resettlement process motivated her to serve as project director for two Title III grants in the Des Moines Public Schools and to teach a variety of graduate classes for educators of ELs. Currently an ESL/diversity consultant at Heartland Area Education Agency, she is a frequent presenter at state, national, and international conferences. Jones-Vo has published numerous articles in magazines and journals and coauthored numerous book chapters. Her first book, coauthored with Shelley Fairbairn, is *Differentiating Instruction and Assessment for English Language Learners: A Guide for K–12 Teachers* (Caslon, 2010).

A corecipient of the Governor's First in the Nation in Education (FINE) Award, Jones-Vo also received the Beyond the Horizon Award for exemplary teaching and advocacy for ELs, and the Governor's Volunteer Award (four times) for service through the Iowa Bureau of Refugee Services. She was recognized with an Outstanding Alumni Award from Drake University in 2010.

The ENGAGE Model

1

An effective driver is a policy (and related strategies) that actually produces better results across the system. An effective driver is not something that sounds plausible; it is not something that can be justified by a cavalier (as distinct from a carefully considered) reference to research. Nor is it an urgent goal (such as moral purpose); rather, drivers that are effective generate a concerted and accelerating force for progress toward the goals of reform. An effective driver is one that achieves better measurable results with students.

(Fullan, 2011a, p. 4)

Fullan sums up what many individual teachers already know; their isolated efforts on behalf of English learners (ELs) cannot result in significant increases in student achievement unless driven by policies and strategies that are collaboratively enacted across their school buildings and districts. When individual teachers collaborate with grade- and building-level colleagues, building/district teams, administrators, and staff by developing mutually supportive relationships and programs that address EL-specific needs, school districts can accelerate their progress in achieving improved measurable results for ELs.

In addition to meeting Fullan's insightful criteria, an effective driver for advancing the achievement of ELs must be rooted, in its essence, in deep understanding of ELs' past and present realities and their specific linguistic, academic, and sociocultural needs. This requires the development of educator knowledge of, and personal connections with, student backgrounds. Such expanded perceptions and relationships constitute the foundation for the empathy and motivation required to implement high-quality instruction and assessment for English learners.

Demographic data reveal that ELs compose the fastest-growing school-aged population in the United States (Mather, 2009, p. 3). Consideration of academic achievement data for these students further reveals the urgent need for an effective driver that will sustain school- and/or district-wide teams and inform their decisions.

OVERVIEW OF THE ENGAGE MODEL

The ENGAGE model represents an effective driver for reform efforts related to the effective instruction and assessment of K–12 English learners, as it

- builds upon a foundation of insights regarding the students served,
- is based upon carefully considered EL-specific research,
- is designed to create a "concerted and accelerating force for progress" on behalf of ELs, and
- will achieve better measurable results with students (Calderón, Slavin, & Sánchez, 2011; EdSource, 2007; Goldenberg, 2008).

An overview of the model is presented in Figure 1.1.

- **E**stablish a shared vision grounded in deep understanding of ELs.
- **N**ame and capitalize upon relevant expertise within collaborative teams.
- **G**ather and analyze EL-specific data.
- **A**lign standards-based assessments and grading with ELs' current levels of linguistic and content development
- **G**round standards-based instruction in both content *and* language development.
- **E**xamine results to inform and drive next steps.

Note that each step in the ENGAGE model builds upon the previous step; a shared vision serves as the foundation for the progression through the steps toward the ultimate goal of increased schoolwide student achievement. Each of these incremental steps is described below.

- To *establish a shared vision for serving ELs*, schools and districts need to first understand and empathize with the backgrounds and stories of the students that they serve. Against this backdrop, educators must then work collaboratively to develop an informed vision for serving these students.
- *Naming the expertise to capitalize upon within collaborative teams* requires that *all* relevant stakeholders be gathered together to identify and

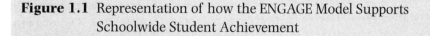

Figure 1.1 Representation of how the ENGAGE Model Supports Schoolwide Student Achievement

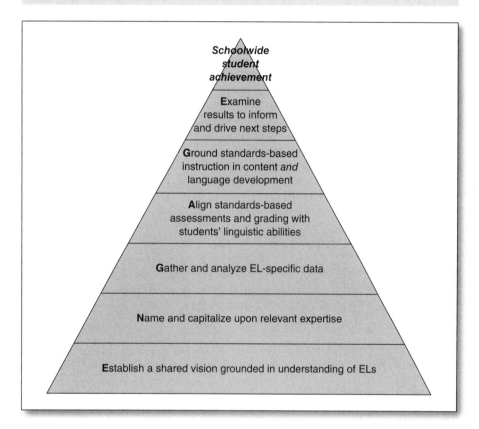

share their individual areas of expertise. Concrete plans are then developed for appropriately incorporating every individual's relevant expertise/experience on behalf of English learners.

- *Gathering and analyzing EL-specific data* requires that, through a critical and EL-specific lens, administrators and teachers interrogate the data that are typically gathered about all students for their relevance and meaning. In addition, they must analyze additional EL data, including relevant classroom-based information, in order to gain the most accurate picture of what ELs know and can do. After interpreting EL-specific data, teachers are better positioned to appropriately conceptualize meaningful linguistic and content-based assignments/assessments.

- *To align standards-based assessments and grading with ELs' current levels of linguistic and content development*, schools and districts must match performance expectations with students' current levels of linguistic capability and content knowledge, skills, and abilities, which facilitates simultaneous growth in both language and content development.

- Once teachers establish appropriate achievement expectations, they are better able to *ground standards-based instruction in both content* and *language development.* Such grounding means that teachers design and implement linguistically differentiated lessons that employ a range of EL-appropriate instructional practices designed to teach content and language simultaneously.
- *Examining results to inform and drive next steps* requires interpretation of EL-specific data collected throughout the teaching/learning process that informs subsequent teacher decision making and actions. This approach is much more effective than (and is preferred to) relying on a preconceived curricular scope and sequence and/or pacing guide.

THE NEED FOR CHANGE

A constellation of local and national factors calls for a radical shift in school practice for English learners in the K–12 setting based on an effective driver, the ENGAGE model. These factors include legal mandates and guidance, a burgeoning K–12 EL population, increasing heterogeneity among ELs, curricular changes, inappropriate/ineffective service delivery for many ELs, and inadequate teacher preparation (see Figure 1.2).

Figure 1.2 Factors That Create the Need for the ENGAGE Model

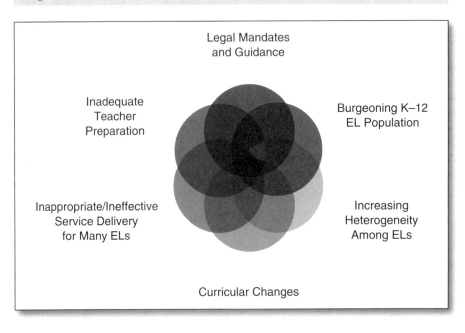

Legal Mandates and Guidance

A number of documents detail the federal requirements for the education of ELs. In 1964, Title VI of the Civil Rights Act declared that

> No person in the United States shall, on the grounds of race, color, or national origin be excluded from participation in, be denied the benefits of, or otherwise be subjected to discrimination under any program or activity receiving federal financial assistance from the Department of Health, Education, and Welfare.

A follow-up memo to the Civil Rights Act (May 25, 1970, Memorandum, Department of Health, Education and Welfare) clarified the responsibility of school districts to provide equal opportunity to students with limited English language proficiency and to ensure that students were not placed in special education programming due simply to a lack of English language proficiency. The Bilingual Education Act, 1968 (amended in 1974 and 1978) encouraged the use of bilingual education and allocated funding to support this programming. The Equal Educational Opportunities Act of 1974 prohibited the denial of student access to educational opportunities based on race, color, sex, or national origin. This act further pointed out the need to specifically address language barriers. These documents set the stage for court decisions that would follow.

In 1974, the Supreme Court ruled in *Lau v. Nichols* that, in terms of educational opportunities, identical is not equal. This ruling further charged districts to take steps to address ELs' linguistic needs. Less than a decade later, *Casteñada v. Pickard* (1981) provided three guidelines for EL programming:

1. Is the program theoretically sound or experimentally appropriate?

2. Is the program set up in a way that allows this theory to be put into practice?

3. Is the program regularly evaluated and adjusted to ensure that it is meeting the linguistic needs of the students it serves?

The following year, in *Plyler v. Doe* (1982), the US Supreme Court struck down the Texas law that allowed school districts to deny educational opportunities to children of undocumented immigrants. This ruling drew upon the Fourteenth Amendment to the US Constitution, perceiving that children, rather than their parents, were effectively punished by such denial. Previously, California, *Diana v. State Board of Education* (1970) had mandated that ELs cannot be placed in special education programming based upon test results that do not separate language proficiency from disability, due to reliance on discriminatory linguistic demands within the test. More recently, the impact of noncompliance findings by the Civil Rights Division of the US Department of Justice and the Office for Civil Rights of the US Department of Education in Massachusetts (Settlement Agreement Between The United States of America and The Boston Public Schools, n.d.) has garnered the attention of states serving ELs. These findings, that some 45,000 general education teachers lacked training to work effectively with ELs, resulted in the requirement for statewide teacher training "developed by language-acquisition experts" (Maxwell, 2012, ¶4).

Early in 2015, the US Department of Justice and the US Department of Education issued joint guidance regarding ways to ensure that ELs can participate "meaningfully and equally in educational programs" (US Department of Justice & US Department of Education, 2015, p. 1). This document serves as a reminder regarding the legal obligations of state education agencies, school districts, and schools by specifically addressing such topics as identification, assessment, programming and program evaluation, staffing, access to curricular and extracurricular opportunities, parent communication, and exit practices. The document makes clear the seriousness of these requirements by concluding with contact information for agencies that address violations of these legal obligations.

The combination of all of the aforementioned legal mandates and guidance documents, arguably illuminates the need for a model of more effective inclusion of ELs in K–12 education. However, the rapidly growing population of English learners still finds itself struggling for access to curriculum.

Burgeoning K–12 EL Population

The United States has seen a significant increase in the number of ELs in recent decades; Haynes (2012, p. 2), points out that "between 1980 and 2009, the number of school-aged children who spoke another language in the home more than doubled, from 4.7 (10 percent) to 11.2 million (21 percent)." More recently, the number of ELs in the United States grew by a stunning 63.54% between academic years 1994–1995 and 2009–2010 (National Clearinghouse for English Language Acquisition [NCELA], 2011a). Further, demographers anticipate that by 2020, "Half of all public school students will have non-English-speaking backgrounds" (Haynes, 2012, p. 2). Individual states and school districts are experiencing a range of EL growth patterns. While some districts are experiencing significant and even overwhelming growth, others are experiencing more gradual changes. Districts with low incidence of ELs, as well as those entirely new to serving ELs, both face daunting challenges. All of these enrollment realities point to the need for a clear-cut and consistent team-based model for engaging ELs in the curriculum. In addition to variable enrollments, the changing composition of the EL population is also notable.

Increasing Heterogeneity Among ELs

The population of ELs across the United States continues to diversify in a phenomenon known as *microplurality,* or "diversity within diversity" (Grey & Devlin, n.d., slide 8). Microplurality, rather than focusing on racial differences, "recognizes the central role of culture, language, religion, and immigration status." For example, language diversity within the United States has increased in recent decades (Shin & Kominski, 2010). While the US Census Bureau listed 325 languages spoken in the United States in 2004, this is likely an underrepresentation, as many languages with few speakers are not reported (National Clearinghouse for English Language Acquisition [NCELA], 2011b). This noteworthy change in diversity of languages spoken across the United States, as well as the increased microplurality visible in culture, religion, and immigration status, has far-reaching implications for instructional approaches, materials, and assessments for ELs. The overarching demographic changes indicate that "business as usual" will not result in increased achievement for all of today's K–12 students. Rather, all stakeholders in the educational process must work together to reconceptualize and implement a model that embraces and meets the distinct academic and sociocultural needs of the full range of English learners. While the K-12 student population is undergoing transformation, the curricula used in K-12 schools are simultaneously changing as well.

Curricular Changes

The untenable achievement gap that persists between ELs and non-ELs (Fry, 2007) demands differentiated instruction and assessment based on EL-specific insights and research. Widely accepted curricular standards such as the Common Core State Standards, with their increased emphasis on rigor, have highlighted the need for such a differentiated approach that ensures effective instruction of *all* students that will afford them parity of access to standards-based achievement. The new standards-based environment provides an unprecedented opportunity for teachers, staff, and administrators to redouble efforts for engaging ELs in grade-level and content classrooms. Implementing a differentiated approach, teachers emphasize the learning of content, as well as its associated academic language, in new and creative ways. This newly envisioned task can be accomplished through a model designed to engage and advance the achievement of diverse learners: the ENGAGE model. Past attempts to facilitate access to curriculum have, all too often, resulted in services for ELs that were not matched with their needs.

Inappropriate/Ineffective Service Delivery for Many ELs

Some districts struggle to distinguish language differences from exceptionalities, resulting in both frequent overrepresentation of ELs in special education programs (Hamayan, Marler, Sanchez-Lopez, & Damico, 2013) and underrepresentation of these students in programs for gifted/talented students (Castellano & Diaz, 2002). In addition, appropriate literacy instruction, which is a critical facilitator of academic success for all students, is often not provided to ELs; current research that illuminates best practice for EL literacy instruction is now available, but the needed modifications to classroom practice have yet to be enacted on a large scale (Goldberg, cited in Linan-Thompson & Vaughn, 2007). These issues with services for ELs have contributed to a dropout rate for ELs that is double that of non-ELs (Callahan, 2013). These disparities contribute to the urgent need for a radical shift in practice through a model designed to engage ELs in all aspects of instruction and assessment. Inappropriate/ ineffective services can be attributed to a number of causes, including inadequate teacher preparation.

Inadequate Teacher Preparation

Insufficient attention has been given to ensuring that all teachers are prepared to effectively teach and assess ELs (Walker & Stone, 2011), despite the fact that most teachers will have ELs in their classrooms (Samson & Collins, 2012). More specifically, in the 2009–2010 academic year, "73 percent [of district EL program administrators] reported that 'lack of expertise among mainstream teachers to address the needs of ELs [English learners]' was a moderate or major challenge" (US Department of Education, Office of Planning, Evaluation and Policy Development, Policy and Program Studies Service, 2012, p. xxvi).

The educational literature recommends that a variety of topics be infused into such teacher preparation. For instance, Staehr Fenner (2013) discusses the necessity of addressing the dual demands of English language proficiency standards layered upon content standards. In addition, a review of the literature reveals that a foundational knowledge base of all teachers of ELs must include oral language development, academic language, and cultural sensitivity (Samson & Collins, 2012, p. 2). Finally, Jones-Vo and Fairbairn (2012, A New Paradigm section, ¶2) emphasize that all teachers who serve ELs must

- Know [their] students
- Increase comprehensibility
- Increase interaction
- Increase higher-order thinking
- Make connections to previous learning
- Differentiate instruction and assessment according to ELP [English language proficiency] levels
- Match grading to differentiated expectations

All of these components combine to promote the simultaneous learning of language and content when conducted collaboratively. Inadequate teacher preparation that fails to include all of these factors has contributed to the need for a new model of EL teaching and assessment practice in the K–12 context.

IMPLEMENTING THE ENGAGE MODEL

The ENGAGE model constitutes a meaningful collaborative response to significant needs of ELs, including the factors described above. This team-based model will serve as an effective driver of districtwide and/or school-wide change that leads to improved EL achievement in the K–12 setting. The ENGAGE model calls upon individual teachers, district/school leaders, and other stakeholders to unify and move forward as productive advocates on behalf of all students and of English learners in particular.

District/school leaders are advised at the outset that, when viewed through the eyes of a single individual, the tasks involved in engaging ELs equitably across an entire district/school could seem daunting. The authors recognize that comprehensive descriptions and summaries of leadership team tasks might seem overwhelming, but only if these tasks are perceived as responsibilities shouldered solely by an individual or by a small leadership group. District/school leaders are encouraged to exhibit shared leadership to distribute responsibilities among all stakeholders, encouraging their contributions in an unlimited variety of ways, such as

- Empowering teacher leaders to work in meaningful ways
- Capitalizing upon existing professional learning community structures to analyze needs and relevant data

- Delegating tasks such as scheduling meetings, collecting information or research, posting documents, and communicating with others
- Seeking input from outside experts, representative first-person voices, and others
- Networking with other districts/schools that are experienced in meeting EL needs
- Participating in relevant professional development
- Adapting the components of the ENGAGE model to match the district- or school-specific context

Through advance planning and widespread distribution of shared responsibilities, district/school leaders will ultimately benefit by streamlining the implementation of the ENGAGE model.

Since these leadership teams will spearhead the implementation of change and refinement in order to engage ELs across the district/school, they must be well versed in the necessary components shouldered by each and every other stakeholder. In order to facilitate such a "balcony view" of individual contexts and roles, the authors have provided descriptions of the ENGAGE model roles across all constituent groups. These descriptions should not intimidate any participants in the implementation process. The authors expect that providing this comprehensive awareness will empower visionary district/school leaders to more seamlessly implement the change process. By sharing a range of tasks and responsibilities at the inception and shouldering the work together, district/school leaders will lighten their individual loads and pave the way for realization of their shared vision. This is meant as encouragement to leaders, so that when previewing the collective and collaborative processes of implementing the ENGAGE model, they recognize the collegial nature and unified spirit inherent in the endeavor.

As district/school leaders consider adopting the ENGAGE model, they are reminded of the iterative nature of this process, and the fact that full implementation will likely take multiple years. The authors have worked with districts/schools at various stages of EL engagement. Such exemplary districts/buildings have been working at fully engaging ELs for a number of years, and constantly refine their work in a cycle of continuous improvement. Exactly how long implementing the ENGAGE model will take depends on many variables within each district/school. Patience and persistence will be key to moving forward as, based on demographic projections, the need to continually refine efforts to engage ELs in standards-based instruction is certain not to diminish. Districts/schools might start by examining and identifying the most important issues at hand, and then, using a backward planning process, break down appropriate next steps. In this way, they can make progress in meaningful, if small, steps.

Ultimately, this book is intended as a field book to be referenced by all stakeholders, but also freely adapted to meet specific school/district needs. Certain steps might be taken out of sequence, if that makes sense for a specific context. The authors hope that this book will be a well-used source of guidance and will provide a common language that will support and unite all stakeholders in accomplishing their shared goal of increasing EL academic achievement. Each chapter of the remainder of this book will explicate one component of the ENGAGE model:

- **E**stablish a shared vision grounded in deep understanding of ELs.
- **N**ame the expertise to capitalize upon within collaborative teams.
- **G**ather and analyze EL-specific data.
- **A**lign standards-based assessments and grading with ELs' current levels of linguistic and content development.
- **G**round standards-based instruction in both content *and* language development.
- **E**xamine results to inform and drive next steps.

Establish a Shared Vision for Serving ELs

2

This is at the heart of creating an equitable school culture: norming difference for students so that each and every one fundamentally knows he or she is loved, accepted, and supported toward excellence, no matter how that student might differ from the educators and other students in the building. An equitable school culture can only exist when the staff as a whole is vested in creating an environment wherein every student succeeds.

(Linton & Davis, 2013, p. xv)

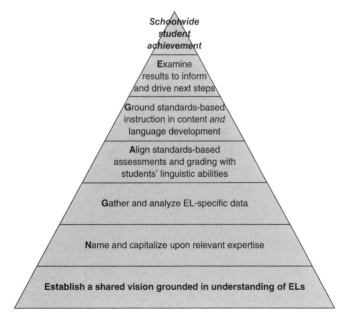

Schoolwide student achievement

Examine results to inform and drive next steps

Ground standards-based instruction in content *and* language development

Align standards-based assessments and grading with students' linguistic abilities

Gather and analyze EL-specific data

Name and capitalize upon relevant expertise

Establish a shared vision grounded in understanding of ELs

Educators must consistently make decisions with a singular question in mind: *Who are our students and what do they need in order to succeed?* The importance of this question cannot be overstated. Furthermore, all stakeholders in the educational process for ELs must play an essential role in answering this question. Such broad-based participation ensures district-/school-wide ownership and enhances the likelihood of comprehensive implementation, which paves the way for increased student achievement. As such, the process of developing a vision statement for serving ELs must be a truly collaborative effort that encompasses the perspectives of all stakeholders and stakeholder groups in the EL educational process. Rather than promoting a predetermined vision, the leaders of shared vision development must embrace the enriching democratic process that negotiating a shared vision entails. Only active involvement and collaboration will result in a vision that can be sustained and enacted over time and that truly articulates the "collective will" of all stakeholders; as Senge and his colleagues clearly state: "Visions based on authority alone are not sustainable" (2012, p. 87). The leader(s) tasked with the development of this vision must convene a lead team that can co-facilitate the process and delegate tasks.

The first order of business in the process of establishing a shared vision is to develop an understanding of the realities of ELs. This foundational understanding of ELs and their cultural, linguistic, and academic starting points drives the development of a common vision. This vision, in turn, drives the actions and decisions of all stakeholders in the English learner educational process (see Figure 2.1).

These actions and decisions constitute the remaining steps of the ENGAGE model, which are grounded in the establishment of a shared vision:

- (**E**stablish a shared vision grounded in deep understanding of ELs.)
- **N**ame and capitalize upon relevant expertise within collaborative teams.
- **G**ather and analyze EL-specific data.
- **A**lign standards-based assessments and grading with ELs' current levels of linguistic and content development.
- **G**round standards-based instruction in both content *and* language development.
- **E**xamine results to inform and drive next steps.

In order to accomplish the "actions and decisions" encompassed by the remaining steps of the ENGAGE model, district-/school-based teams will

Figure 2.1 Implementation of the ENGAGE Model

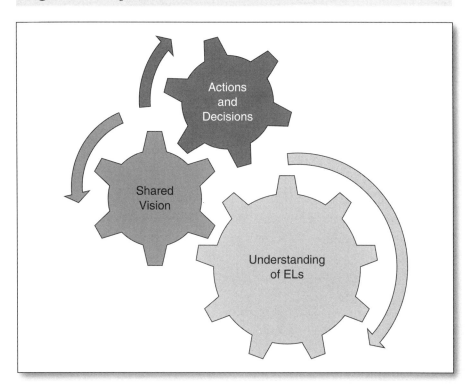

participate in a wide variety of activities on behalf of ELs. These activities are described in detail throughout the remainder of the book and include

- conversations (Chapters 2–7),
- lesson planning (Chapter 6),
- materials selection and adoptions (Chapter 6),
- curricular decisions (Chapter 5),
- resource allocations (Chapters 2–7),
- interventions (Chapter 6),
- program development and implementation (Chapters 2–7),
- assessment development, selection, and implementation (Chapter 5),
- grading (Chapter 5), and
- review of results to refine the implementation of the ENGAGE Model (Chapter 7), among others.

These activities and decisions must be grounded in the shared vision, which is the focus of this chapter. Developing a district-/school-wide understanding of English learners and their cultural, linguistic, and academic needs informs the creation of a shared vision which, in turn, drives all school-based decisions that impact ELs.

OVERVIEW OF THE VISION DEVELOPMENT PROCESS

> *The first and biggest idea . . . is that the fundamental purpose of schools is to ensure that all students learn as distinct from all students should be taught. This will require the development of shared goals and vision, the alignment of procedures and practices, and specific indicators of progress.*

> (Fullan, 2011b, p. 4)

Fullan asserts unequivocally that the purpose of schools is to ensure the learning of *all* students. This purpose is best accomplished through the development and implementation of a shared vision, facilitated by a lead team, which carries out the following steps:

- Establish norms for lead team members
- Identify all appropriate stakeholders
- Plan the meeting schedule and location
- Convene stakeholders
- Establish norms for the group
- Enact the vision planning and writing process, in which the group must
  - Coconstruct "a clear picture of the current reality" (Senge et al., 2012, p. 88).
    - Explore the heterogeneity of the students and their distinct EL background characteristics.
    - Gain input from each relevant stakeholder group.
  - Coconstruct "a clear statement of the desired outcomes ('what we want to create together')" (Senge et al., 2012, p. 88).
    - Gain input from each relevant stakeholder group.
    - Categorize and prioritize ideas about desired outcomes.
    - Write the vision statement, incorporating all stakeholder input.
    - Gather public comments.
    - Submit to relevant leaders for final approval.
  - Coconstruct "a collective choice about how to proceed" (Senge et al., 2012, p. 88).
    - Based on finalized vision statement, identify potential barriers to success (Bainbridge, 2007).
    - Determine action steps (Bainbridge, 2007).

- Communicate the final vision and action steps
- Support stakeholders in enacting the vision
- Acknowledge, celebrate, and reward efforts

Throughout the process of vision development, team leaders must facilitate effective communication and ensure that ideas from all stakeholders are heard. Each step in the visioning process is detailed below. Districts/schools are encouraged to use Resource 2.1 at the end of the chapter to plan their work on each of these steps.

ESTABLISH NORMS FOR LEAD TEAM MEMBERS

Due to the complex nature of leading change, which can include such challenging activities as addressing contentious issues and resolving conflict, leaders must "learn and employ [strategies or methods] that will increase their ability to lead change" (Knight, 2007, p. 198). Knight suggests eight "high-leverage leadership tactics" (p. 198) that can be utilized to enhance the efficacy of lead team members (p. 196):

- Protecting yourself by staying detached
- Being prepared by walking on solid ground
- Communicating clearly by clarifying your message
- Meeting teachers' needs by managing change effectively
- Facing facts by confronting reality
- Making fundamental improvements by understanding school culture
- Leading by being ambitious and humble
- Staying energized by taking care of yourself

This structure, among others, can provide the means for lead team members to successfully facilitate change. Once the lead team has established norms, it can move to the next step in the development of a shared vision for serving ELs.

IDENTIFY ALL APPROPRIATE STAKEHOLDERS

The development of a robust shared vision depends upon the district's/school's response to the following question: Who exactly are the stakeholders in the achievement of ELs? The more specificity that districts/schools express in terms of the composition of this group, the more stakeholders they will list. Responsive, student-centered districts/schools may likely include the following participants in the EL-specific vision development process: school board members; district/building administrators; instructional leaders/coaches; curriculum specialists; school counselors; EL and classroom/content teachers; food service, custodial, transportation, and office staff; paraeducators; parents; community members; and students. Individual districts/schools may well include additional stakeholders (e.g., city librarian, mayor).

PLAN THE MEETING SCHEDULE AND LOCATION

Each district/school will determine the best way to gain input from all stakeholder groups. In some cases, various groups may meet separately (e.g., Bainbridge, 2007). In other contexts, representatives of each stakeholder group may attend each and every meeting. Stakeholder schedules, particularly those of EL parents, must be considered in order to facilitate representative participation in the process. Organizers should also recognize that various supports will likely enhance attendance and participation of some EL parents and students (e.g., transportation to and from meetings, refreshments, child care during meetings, language interpretation, personal invitations extended to parents and students by phone or in person).

CONVENE STAKEHOLDERS

Districts/schools will meet with stakeholders in accordance with their individual needs based on the schedule developed by the lead team, in accordance with stakeholder availability.

ESTABLISH NORMS FOR THE GROUP

"Work in groups is often difficult, filled with conflicts and tensions, but it is also absolutely necessary for achieving results in modern organizations" (Garmston & Wellman, 2013, p. 27). Establishing a set of commonly understood norms can facilitate the challenging work of developing a shared vision for serving ELs. One versatile framework for productive interactions adopted by many district/school groups is "The Seven Norms of Collaboration" (Garmston & Wellman, 2013, p. 31):

1. Pausing

2. Paraphrasing

3. Posing questions

4. Putting ideas on the table

5. Providing data

6. Paying attention to self and others

7. Presuming positive intentions

Districts/schools may elect to adopt such a proven set of norms or establish their own.

ENACT THE VISION PLANNING AND WRITING PROCESS

As Ghiso astutely states, "When the education of ELLs becomes the priority of the school as a whole, we can more successfully foster the engagement and continued growth of students who are often forgotten by the system" (2012, pp. 185–186). Developing a shared vision will position ELs front and center, illuminating ways to enhance their academic success. This collaborative effort takes place through a series of steps.

Step 1: Coconstruct "a clear picture of the current reality" (Senge et al., 2012, p. 88)

The fast-growing and increasingly diverse population of ELs in the United States "has not fared well in U.S. schools . . . despite forty years of federal investment in programs for English learners" (Haynes, 2012, p. 3). However, "Ensuring that English language learners receive an education that prepares them for life after high school must be a priority for communities and states. Meeting this challenge is both urgent and daunting" (p. 16).

In order to meet this challenge, individual districts/schools must recognize the urgency and importance of fully engaging ELs in every aspect of school life, from core curriculum to extracurricular activities. In addition, districts/schools must take steps to educate stakeholders about the real students in their midst and the circumstances that define their realities.

Explore the Heterogeneity of the Students and Their Distinct EL Characteristics

The student vignettes below illustrate vast variability among ELs, which must inform the development of a student-centered shared vision.

Chandra is a 9-year-old Bhutanese refugee who was born in a refugee camp in Nepal. Her first language is Nepali, though she can only read and write this language (which uses the Devanagari script) minimally, since she attended an English-medium school in the camp. (Her parents taught her basic reading and writing in Nepali.) Her current school district is unable to ascertain her listening and speaking abilities in her first language due to a lack of appropriate first-language assessments. She and her family practice the Hindu religion, adhering to a caste system and specific gender roles. They also abstain from eating beef. Further, in contrast to many of her current third-grade classmates, she was raised to think of others before herself and to consider what might benefit her family in all decisions.

This Bhutanese family, who has been in the United States for one year, consists of Chandra, her parents, her maternal grandparents, her aunt and uncle, and their three children. They share a small, three-bedroom apartment in a run-down complex in a declining neighborhood inhabited largely by refugee families from around the globe. Paying for rent and other expenses is a challenge, as only Chandra's father and uncle are working (at a large discount store), and her grandfather is quite ill. In fact, Chandra is pulled out of school on a regular basis to interpret at his medical appointments. This interpretation is quite limited, however, by her own initial proficiency in English (which has not grown since her arrival): Level 3 in speaking and listening, Level 2 in reading, and Level 1 in writing.

Support for her English development at home is limited to watching TV and interacting with other diverse children who speak a variety of first languages. Chandra loves to spend time outdoors with these friends and, when supplies are handy, enjoys sketching pictures of flowers, trees, and nature. Her teachers have referred Chandra for special education, as some large-scale tests have labeled her to be "significantly discrepant" from her peers. The referral process is stalled at the moment, though, as there is no one available to interpret the meetings and translate documents for her parents. (No first language support has been available to Chandra or her family by the district since she arrived.)

Vincente is a 12-year-old seventh-grade boy from Mexico who was born in a small village south of Mexico City. He lives with his uncle (with whom he immigrated to the United States last month), an aunt and uncle and two cousins (whom he had not met before coming to the United States), and his elderly grandmother. Vincente is obeying his parents' wish that he come to the United States for improved educational and employment opportunities. Despite his upbringing that honors the importance of "family first," he struggles with loneliness and resentment and just wants to "go home." His only outlet is playing soccer with neighborhood youth.

The family's small house is located in a neighborhood inhabited entirely by immigrants from Mexico and Central America. His first language is Spanish, which shares an alphabet with English. However, at enrollment, his first language reading and writing skills were determined to be at the second-grade level, due to the three years that he was not enrolled in school in Mexico, as reported by his uncle. However, intake assessments reveal that his social language in Spanish is appropriate for a typical seventh grader. (It is anticipated that his academic language in Spanish is well below that, although many teachers may incorrectly assume that his level of academic language in Spanish mirrors his high level of social language.)

Vincente's level of English proficiency is beginning (Level 1) in listening, speaking, reading, and writing. Although his aunt and uncle both have a strong command of English (much needed in their work in their restaurant in a nearby suburb), only Spanish is spoken in the home out of respect for Grandma. As a result, Vincente is exposed to English only via TV and at school.

During his first month at school, Vincente's behavior has caused problems for him; he was taken to the principal for fighting in the cafeteria last week and again this week for throwing a dictionary during a social studies test.

Marco is a 15-year-old ninth grader from Brazil. He came to the United States six months ago with his bilingual parents and three-year-old sister when his father was hired to lead a large international engineering firm. His mother is the first chair violinist in the local symphony. (Marco's older brother was already living in the United States, attending a prestigious university.) They reside in a wealthy suburb in a palatial home. In some ways, Marco is culturally similar to many of his American peers, as he has an individualistic, competitive attitude and prefers to work alone (rather than collaboratively).

Marco's first language is Portuguese, which shares the Roman script with English. His first language skills are evidently quite strong, as indicated by his stellar report card from Brazil combined with his father's statement that Marco was at the top of his class at a large high school. His English skills are strong as well, thanks to private English classes and private tutoring back in Brazil. He scored at Level 5 in listening and Level 4 in speaking, reading, and writing. Due to advocacy and pressure exerted by Marco's parents, he has been identified for gifted/talented services. Further, at his own request, Marco does not participate in English as a second language programming. In his spare time, he enjoys practicing the cello. He plans to audition for the symphony next year.

(Continued)

(Continued)

Jessica is also 15 years old and in ninth grade. However, she was born in the United States to immigrants from Mexico. Her father works as part of a construction crew, and her mother is a full-time homemaker, leaving the socioeconomic status of the family quite low. Jessica has two brothers, age three and eight, and two sisters, ages five and twelve, and they live in a three-bedroom apartment in a building inhabited entirely by Spanish-speaking residents. (Neither of her parents speaks English.) As a result, Jessica does not use much English outside of school. She helps her mother in the home before and after school and takes responsibility for some child-rearing tasks, maintaining the family-focused collectivistic culture of her parents. As part of this culture, her family makes annual trips to Mexico to see relatives when they can afford it, even though these trips put Jessica even further behind in her school work.

Jessica's first language is Spanish, though she cannot read and write very well in that language, given that she has not received consistent bilingual services. Although she has attended English-medium schools since kindergarten, her listening and speaking levels are both 4, and her reading and writing levels are both 3, due to inadequate instruction to support her development of academic English. Her progress in learning has been stagnant for several years, her content learning has stalled, and some of her teachers consider her to be lazy. She aspires to be a nurse one day and looks forward to attending community college, though the remedial classes in which she has been placed are not preparing her for this kind of postsecondary educational experience. Though she is pleasant and personable, due to her lack of academic English, Jessica is not passing general science and is destined to retake it, rather than moving on higher level science classes.

These student vignettes highlight the heterogeneity of English learners. Each of the aforementioned students is distinctively unique across a range of background characteristics. A number of researchers have pointed out that the terms "English learner" or "English language learner" (ELL) are problematic, as they tend to over look these many background characteristics (Galguera, 2011, pp. 86–87):

> Scholars have argued that the ELL designation elicits deficit views that ignore the students' wealth of experiences (Marx, 2002), social and cultural capital (Valdes, 1996), cultural background (Moll, 1992; Montero-Siebruthe & Batt, 2001), and prior schooling (Callahan, 2005), among other variables. Further, an emphasis on a lack of English proficiency can elicit deficit thinking among teachers (Valencia, 1997), but especially beginning teachers, who

often view ELL students as lacking English proficiency, intellectual abilities, content knowledge, or even motivation and respect (Wade, Fauske, & Thompson, 2008, p. 431).

While various systems require the use of designations such as EL or ELL, educators will benefit from a closer examination of a range of learner background characteristics in order to understand the strengths and needs of their students and the ways that these strengths and needs can drive instructional design. Each of these characteristics can inform and differentially impact the teaching/learning process of individual students, necessitating instructional approaches or interventions grounded in individual student data (see Chapter 3). In other words, a one-size-fits-all response to EL needs implemented solely on the basis of a single test score can be expected to be inappropriate and insufficient to meet individual student needs.

An abacus serves as a useful metaphor for English learners (see Figure 2.2).

Each student's background characteristics are unique, as represented by the variable position of the beads on each rung of the abacus. Not only

Figure 2.2 Representation of Varying Student Backgrounds

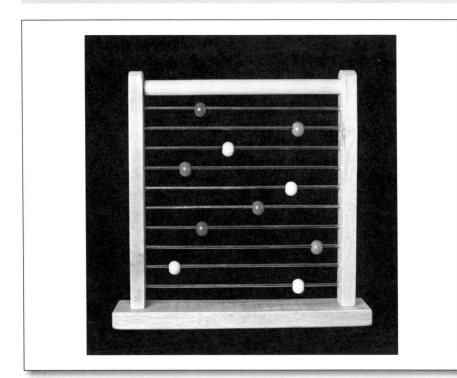

are there many characteristics to consider (the rungs), but there is variability within each characteristic along a continuum (indicated by the position of the bead). These EL background characteristics, the variability within them, and their associated impacts on the teaching/learning process include, but may not be limited to, the following:

- Age
- Grade
- Family background
- Country of origin/country of domicile
- Immigrant/refugee/migrant/other status
- Living situation
- Socioeconomic status
- Cultural background/practices
- Educational backgrounds/content knowledge, skills, and abilities
- First language/script
- First language listening/speaking levels
- First language reading/writing levels
- Length of time in the United States
- English listening/speaking levels
- English reading/writing levels
- Exposure to English outside of school
- Other factors (e.g., gifted/talented, special education, physical disabilities)
- Student interests

We describe each of these background characteristics in detail in subsequent paragraphs.

AGE

The younger the age at which students can engage in grade-level content learning and English language development, the smaller the content and language achievement gaps they need to close. As a result, younger English learners (such as Chandra in the vignette above) are better positioned with more time to catch up to grade-level peers. Nevertheless, educators must realize the value and advantage of consistent language-focused instruction experienced by native-English-speaking third graders over time, such as reading books that are based on children's song lyrics, that Chandra has missed to this point as a nine-year-old child. In order to make multiple years' progress in one year, students like Chandra will require targeted, purposeful, and consistent English language development opportunities in each domain (listening, speaking, reading, and writing) that take into account their individual cultural, linguistic, and academic characteristics. This type of culturally and linguistically sensitive content-based language instruction must occur for all ELs who, like Chandra, demonstrate gaps across a range of skills, particularly those ELs in upper grades.

These older students (such as Marco in the vignette above) have been described as shouldering "double the work" in learning larger amounts of both language and content in a shorter timeframe (Short & Fitzsimmons, 2007). However, Marco has the great advantage of advanced reading and writing skills in his first language. His linguistic skills and metacognitive strategies are, indeed, transferrable when learning English. As a result, Marco could be expected to advance at a faster rate (though he has more ground to cover in terms of catching up to peers who are on grade level in the content areas). Students like Marco, though very committed to learning and independent in their approach, will still need teacher support to meet this dual challenge.

Jessica, though exposed to content curriculum since kindergarten, has not mastered academic language and is in need of specialized programming tailored to her needs, including English language development targeting her specific linguistic needs (which differ from those of ELs who have not been in US schools for a number of years) and access to grade-level classes that serve heterogeneous student populations, among other things (Olsen, 2010). Given that Jessica is a long-term EL like Marco, programming appropriate for Marco would not be appropriate for her, despite their similar levels of English language proficiency.

GRADE

While schools need to follow local guidelines for appropriate grade-level placement for ELs (e.g., within two years of their grade-level peers), there is not necessarily a match between their assigned grade level and their English language development level, nor, in particular, their reading level and content knowledge and skills in English. In the vignettes above, both Chandra and Vincente are reading at levels far below their current grade-level placements. Such data must be considered when planning programming for ELs, in order to appropriately and effectively develop their English language skills.

In another example, imagine a 12-year-old child placed in seventh grade who has not yet developed literacy skills in her first language and is in the beginning stage of learning English. In her case, the grade place-ment would be determined solely by her age. Critical to understanding this student's instructional needs, educators must recognize that her age-appropriate grade-level placement does not take into account her specific learning needs, which must also be addressed intentionally and with a specific plan. This student requires access to grade-level content based on her ability to engage in English, which, by definition, is at a lower level than that of her native-English-speaking classmates. Providing this equity of access to curriculum demands team-based understanding that such instruction should not be considered remediation; this student has never before received such targeted instruction in English. Further, many pro-grams and their associated materials designed for "struggling" students are unlikely to be appropriate for this child; she is not a "struggling learner." Words such as "significantly discrepant" do not apply to her and should also be avoided. If comparisons with other students with similar cultural and linguistic backgrounds reveal her achievement to be far below that of those peers, other background characteristics must be explored. It is possible that she is, in fact, performing at her developmen-tally appropriate threshold of linguistic capability. If this is the case, she is simply in need of meaningful and comprehensible learning opportunities matched with her English language development level, as evidenced by her data. She needs the opportunity to learn and practice English (listen-ing, speaking, reading, *and* writing) for the first time, as her native-Eng-lish-speaking peers have already experienced throughout their lifetimes. Note that opportunities to learn and practice English for the first time (even if that means learning to read from the very beginning) should not be determined for ELs based solely on grade level; all ELs must be afforded appropriate English language instruction matching their current needs, regardless of grade-level placement.

FAMILY BACKGROUND

The importance of knowing a student's family background cannot be understated. While some students benefit from the support of extended families (e.g., Chandra, in the vignette above), others are separated from loved ones (e.g., Vincente, in the vignette above) and may even be living alone. While research suggests that parental involvement is asso-ciated with higher student achievement (Fan & Chen, 2001), families may not know how to support their children's school-based learning. As could be expected, ELs who lack any familial support whatsoever are at an even greater disadvantage. School-based teams can and must reach out to students and families (e.g., home visits, bilingual communication) to ensure that students have needed support, or, if students don't have family support, to provide it by making connections between home and school. Further, schools must develop policies that take into consideration the specific needs of individual ELs (e.g., a high school student living alone who is expected to obtain parental permission for a school activity).

COUNTRY OF ORIGIN/COUNTRY OF DOMICILE

Understanding an EL's country of origin (and countries of domicile, if different), is essential for school-based teams, though it is at times complicated. Some ELs spend their entire lives in a single country prior to immigrating to the United States (e.g., Marco, who is on or above grade level in Brazil). Alternatively, some children may have been born in a given country but spent much of their lives in a second country prior to coming to the United States (e.g., a Sudanese child who lived for several years in Egypt may speak Arabic in addition to a tribal language, such as Dinka, Nuer, or Mabaan).

In yet another example, the birthplace of some ELs may not represent their nationality. For example, Chandra (in the vignette above) was born in a refugee camp in Nepal to Bhutanese parents. She is not considered to be a Nepali national, though she lived her entire life in Nepal where refugees from Bhutan were not welcomed. Rather, as a refugee, Chandra is considered to be Bhutanese, even though she has never set foot in Bhutan. This student may exhibit more Bhutanese cultural norms (e.g., folk medical practices) than those of Nepal, since she was forced to live in a closed camp with other Bhutanese refugees. In addition, she may likely exhibit the culture of the refugee camp (e.g., taking resources for her own as soon as they become available).

The largest group of ELs in the United States was actually born in this country (Batalova, Fix, & Murray, 2007) and are US citizens, as is the case of Jessica in the vignette above. However, these students do not always learn sufficient English to exit English language development programs within the four to seven years that Hakuta, Butler, & Witt (2000) assert to be the time needed to master academic English. As such, students like Jessica earn the label of long-term English learners (LTELs) (Olsen, 2010).

In summary, ELs are likely to be impacted by each place where they have spent time. Knowing about where the child has lived can yield meaningful insights to inform school-based teams' decision making about EL programming and instruction.

IMMIGRANT/REFUGEE/MIGRANT/OTHER STATUS

Fortunately, schools are charged to educate all of the children who come to their doors; thanks to a number of legal mandates (see Chapter 1), school-based teams can focus on enrolling and teaching students, rather than assuming the role of US Immigration and Customs Enforcement (ICE). Further, as noted above, the majority of ELs in US schools were actually born in the United States (Batalova, Fix, & Murray, 2007). Regardless, teams who understand the conditions under which students come to their schools will be able to better tailor programming and supports.

An immigrant generally arrives in the United States of her or his own accord (though often for very compelling reasons), while a refugee is defined as

> a person who is outside his or her country of nationality or habitual residence; has a well-founded fear of persecution because of his or her race, religion, nationality, membership of a particular social group or political opinion; and is unable or unwilling to avail himself or herself of the protection of that country, or to return there, for fear of persecution. (United Nations High Commissioner for Refugees [UNHCR], 2007, p. 6)

In the earlier vignettes, Marco and Vincente represent immigrants, while Chandra is classified as a refugee. While Marco and his family have come through legal channels, Vincente represents the many undocumented children in US schools. Chandra and her family, as refugees, have received documentation from the UNHCR in cooperation with the US Congress.

In yet another example, students who come from migrant families engaged in temporary seasonal agricultural work have specific instructional needs related to their frequently interrupted education, cultural and language differences, and social isolation (e.g., a student may attend school in a given district only for a few months while his parents harvest a seasonal crop, resulting in fragmented learning opportunities and no sense of belonging within the school). In addition, migrant students may qualify the district for additional funding and resources designed to support the children of such temporary agricultural workers. Becoming familiar with qualifications and descriptions of such resources will help districts best meet the needs of migrant students by maximizing access to needed supports. School-based teams need to understand how to identify, report, and assist migrant students and families in their districts.

No matter how any student eventuates in a US classroom, educators are charged with becoming fully informed about each student's background characteristics and assuming responsibility for providing parity of access to the curriculum in their specific contexts.

LIVING SITUATION

As is the case with the aforementioned background characteristics, a student's living situation can positively or negatively impact learning. While Marco enjoys a lighted study area in his own large bedroom and experiences high parental expectations and guidance for homework completion, Chandra, Vincente, and Jessica have no access to a dedicated study area, due to space limitations and cultural norms. (In some cultures, the notion of privacy literally does not translate; providing a solitary study space for students from such cultural groups could be contrary to the cultural norm of togetherness emphasized in their collectivistic communities.) In addition, these three students are expected to spend their time after school engaged in activities that support their families (e.g., babysitting for younger cousins, assisting an ill grandparent, preparing meals, interpreting at doctor or legal appointments). Further, non-English-speaking families can be unlikely to be able to assist students with homework. Clearly, various living situations impact EL learning and should inform team-based decision making (e.g., homework policies).

SOCIOECONOMIC STATUS

The EL population cuts a broad swath across the range of socioeconomic backgrounds, from high poverty to extreme wealth. In the same way that socioeconomic status impacts non-ELs' school-based achievement, so it adds a layer of complexity to knowing ELs. For example, while they can be assured that Marco has every material need met, educators should, on the other hand, be fully aware of the needs of students like Chandra. Despite attempts to pool resources within her extended family, Chandra suffers from food insecurity and has been known to go without meals on the weekend. In addition, she doesn't own a backpack, but carries her limited school supplies (a pencil and a single notebook) to and from school in a plastic bag. She is apprehensive about the upcoming science fair, as she is about many assignments, as her family cannot afford to buy special craft materials to create a project or to compete with other students.

Perceptive and concerned teachers can assist students like Chandra in several ways. With regard to her food insecurity, they might help her to enroll in the free- and reduced-price lunch and breakfast programs at school. In addition, informed school-based teams can develop creative ways to ensure that students have food to eat on Saturday and Sunday (e.g., food backpacks provided by a parent–teacher organization). These school-based teams can also seek out funding for a school store of materials, or donations from businesses, that students in need can access for project-based work.

CULTURAL BACKGROUND/PRACTICES

ELs enrich US classrooms with a wide variety of cultural backgrounds and practices. While supporting students in acquiring the cultural competence needed for success in the United States, teachers must embrace the fact that "every individual has the right to maintain his or her own identity while acquiring the skills required to function in our diverse society" (Early Head Start Resource Center @ ZERO TO THREE, n.d., p. 41). Conversely, teachers share a responsibility to develop the cultural competence needed to interact successfully with students and families different from themselves. One useful continuum for understanding cultural difference is that of individualism and collectivism (Ting-Toomey & Chung, 2005, 2011), which ranges from cultures that are highly individualistic and competitive to those that are focused predominantly on group interaction, success, and harmony. School-based teams need to be able to adopt and interpret interactions with students and families through a culturally informed lens to build relationships that will support student learning.

School-based teams can build relationships with ELs and their families by respectfully integrating varied cultural backgrounds and practices into the classroom. For example, since Chandra comes from a modest culture that may not support her participation in a swimming class, culturally competent school team members can collaborate to develop alternative ways for Chandra to participate in physical education (e.g., a different sports activity, a swimming class for girls only). Likewise, her abstinence from beef must be respected; food service personnel, in collaboration with other members of the school-based team, can provide clearly labeled nonbeef alternatives at lunch and keep Chandra informed of these options. Creating a welcoming environment where students and families feel that their unique characteristics and situations are known, honored, and respected helps to set the stage for academic achievement. Incorporating the unified district/school collective will to equitably integrate ELs' needs into every aspect of school life, including food service and transportation, supports these students in feeling secure and safe in their schools, paving the way to EL academic engagement.

EDUCATIONAL BACKGROUNDS/CONTENT KNOWLEDGE, SKILLS, AND ABILITIES

Educational background is a characteristic that often has the most significant impact on school-based learning. Students like Marco, who are on or above grade level in their first language, will require a far different instructional approach than students such as Vincente and Chandra, who have gaps in first language (L1) educational backgrounds. Students like Jessica, who have not mastered academic English due to inadequate instruction, are sometimes viewed as simply unmotivated or lazy. School-based teams must analyze exactly which instructional gaps exist (even if the EL has attended school consistently from a young age) in order to engage these students at their current instructional levels. Assessments in the student's L1, or assessments devoid of language, may be used for this purpose. In other cases, teachers themselves will determine the content knowledge, skills, and abilities of their ELs through observation, classroom activities, and/or formative assessment.

Due to their lack of both literacy and grade-level content instruction in their first languages, both Vincente and Chandra have significantly greater instructional needs than Marco. As a result, they will require even more explicit background building, EL-specific early literacy and oral language development strategies, focused vocabulary development, academic language instruction and practice, and regular embedded interaction opportunities to practice English with peers. It will be important to routinely engage Chandra and Vincente, just like Marco and native-English-speaking students, in higher order thinking tasks, even while they are performing at lower levels of English language development. Jessica, too, needs opportunities to interact with native speakers of English, though the gaps in her content knowledge, skills, and abilities are, sadly, the result of her inadequate schooling experiences in the United States. Programming for Jessica must be tailored to her specific needs; neither remedial classes for native speakers of English nor English language development classes for students who have arrived in the United States in recent years would be appropriate for Jessica.

FIRST LANGUAGE/SCRIPT

Students like Marco, Vincente, and Jessica, whose first language mirrors English in using Roman script, are at a distinct advantage over students whose first language scripts differ, in a variety of ways. For example, Chandra's first language script, Devanagari, is very different from English script. Though she reads and writes minimally in Nepali (using Devanagari script), her beginning-level writing in English is also minimal, leaving her with specific needs, including literacy development that emphasizes oral language development. It must be noted that Chandra's beginning-level proficiency in first language reading and writing offers some support to her in the development of second-language (L2) literacy, but that students with higher levels of L1 literacy experience this transfer to a higher degree (Cummins, 2001). Also, since Chandra is only beginning to write in English, she needs continued instruction on letter formation, particularly as she further develops her sense of letter–sound correspondence. Teams who identify EL instructional gaps and needs, regardless of the student's grade level, can readily collaborate to meet those needs intentionally and to monitor student progress.

FIRST LANGUAGE LISTENING/SPEAKING LEVELS

When considering the development of listening and speaking skills in the first language, the onset of social language generally precedes the development of academic language. All four of the focal students in the vignettes above can be considered to have reasonable levels of proficiency in social communication skills in the first language. However, in terms of academic language, only Marco would be considered to be on grade level in the L1; Chandra, Vincente, and Jessica did not receive first-language grade-level instruction sufficient for the development of academic language at their current grade levels. As a result, such language has not become embedded into their L1 speaking repertoire and therefore cannot transfer into their speaking in English. Bearing this in mind, teachers must recognize that social language development in English constitutes a bridge to academic language development in English; teachers must consistently embed opportunities for students to build academic language upon their growing foundation of social language skills. Focusing on essential academic language development will be an essential task of school-based teams who have cultivated a collective vision, as will holding ELs accountable for producing academic vocabulary and discourse in the classroom.

FIRST LANGUAGE READING/WRITING LEVELS

With the exception of Marco, the focal students in this chapter perform well below grade level in their ability to both read and write in their first languages. Fortunately, a Spanish-language assessment is available for use in determining Vincente's L1 reading and writing levels (second grade in both cases). Jessica's L1 reading and writing have not been evaluated for years, as she is no longer able to access bilingual programming and is considered by some of her teachers to just be lazy, since she has attended US schools since kindergarten. Unfortunately, as is the case for many ELs, there is no L1 assessment available for use in determining Chandra's reading and writing level in her L1. Even a discussion of her proficiency is impossible, as there are no interpreters available in her school district to assist in gaining insights from her parents. Since Chandra's L1 writing skill is limited and employs non-Roman script, she is unable to directly transfer significant reading and writing skills from Nepali to English. While research bears out the value of first teaching students to read and write in their L1 (Snow, Burns, & Griffin, 1998), this is not an option for Chandra. Students such as Chandra represent an urgent need for literacy instruction that will accelerate their academic success and position them for graduation and career readiness.[1] To support this goal, the team-based vision for ELs should embody a philosophy that honors and preserves their heritage languages, enabling students to communicate with elders and others in their L1 community.[2] Such an additive philosophy welcomes and encourages interactions in the L1, such as reading books to children at home, as a means of supporting literacy and academic achievement in English. At the same time, administrators must ensure a vigorous district-/schoolwide response that includes willing, qualified, and dedicated teachers, along with appropriately differentiated resources.

LENGTH OF TIME IN THE UNITED STATES

In terms of English language development, how long an EL has lived in the United States is less informative than whether the EL has received quality instruction, as Jessica's case highlights. That is, longer periods of time in the United States do not necessarily correlate with higher levels of English language development. For example, while Marco is progressing according

---

[1]It is noted that many ELs work part time and even full time while in school.

[2]Wong-Fillmore (2000) describes the communication breakdowns that can result from teachers' insistence that EL families speak only English.

to grade-level expectations thanks to his L1 preparation, parental support and tutoring, and his variety of advantageous background characteristics, Vincente is following a different trajectory. Unless he receives engaging, team-based, and visionary EL services, Vincente is at risk for not fully developing his English skills, not reaching his full potential, and dropping out of school, since he feels overwhelmed by the academic and reading demands of his seventh-grade classes. Again, the focus must be on ensuring that content and language instruction is geared to match the individual needs of ELs such as Vincente.

ENGLISH LISTENING/SPEAKING LEVELS

As is the case with L1 development, social language generally develops prior to academic language in the L2. This language acquisition process is incremental and predictable. It occurs gradually, over time, and follows a trajectory that is often described as broken into specific levels, each with a description of what students know and can do in English. For example, Teachers of English to Speakers of Other Languages (TESOL) delineates five such levels: Level 1—Starting, Level 2—Emerging, Level 3—Developing, Level 4—Expanding, and Level 5—Bridging (TESOL, 2006b). Further, first language development serves to support second language development. For this reason, Marco, with his advanced proficiency in both Portuguese and English, is at a distinct advantage over Chandra, Vincente, and Jessica. These three students lack academic listening and speaking skills in both languages. They will likely require more time to catch up with peers who are on grade level in English than Marco, even though Chandra and Vincente are younger than he is.

ENGLISH READING/WRITING LEVELS

The development of reading and writing skills in English is a time-consuming endeavor that impacts learning in all subject areas; ELs with limited literacy skills in English will struggle in all subjects that require reading and writing. Even ELs who come to the United States with advanced skills in English may perform below grade-level expectations in both reading and writing. This is an expected reality; the use of terms such as *deficient* or *discrepant* to describe these students is inappropriate and unnecessarily negative. Viewed through the lens of research on second language acquisition (e.g., Hakuta, Butler, & Witt, 2000), these students are predictably on target in terms of their linguistic development. Determining "discrepancy" can be done accurately only in light of a truly representative norm group (e.g., ELs with the same background characteristics who have been the United States for the same length of time and have received similar kinds of instruction). While it is difficult to find a representative norm group for most ELs, comparing them to native-English-speaking peers is, at best, unfair; at worst, it results in inappropriate programming, mismatched instruction, and a failure to meet the real needs of ELs. As Popham (2014, p. 64) articulates, "To support actionable instructional decisions about how to best teach students, *norm-referenced inferences simply don't cut it*" (emphasis in original). This is never more evident than when trying to apply instructional strategies designed for native speakers of English to ELs.

Teachers must be prepared to deliver targeted instruction in reading and writing development to all ELs, regardless of their various starting points. Knowing which literacy skills ELs bring to the classroom provides clear guidance for teachers on where to begin their instruction. Team-based implementation of English reading and writing instruction for ELs must be carried out with the same relentless intensity, regularity, and purpose that was afforded native speakers of English as they developed beginning literacy from very young ages.

EXPOSURE TO ENGLISH OUTSIDE OF SCHOOL

Every interaction in English can reinforce the EL's ability to navigate the world in English. Some ELs have frequent opportunities to practice their English both inside and outside of school, while others depend exclusively on school. While some ELs such as Marco travel the world in wide circles offering frequent opportunities to practice English at home, in restaurants, at social events, and with peers, Vincente and Jessica are more confined by their smaller environments, where all family members speak Spanish, and their enclave communities, where all neighbors, even from different countries, also speak Spanish. School is the primary place where Vincente and Jessica practice English, produce the sounds of English, and try out words. Due to the powerful impact of increased opportunity to use English, every teacher in every classroom must routinely embed opportunities for student interactions that incorporate both social and academic language. School-based teams must collaborate to ensure that those who have no opportunities to use English outside of school experience embedded opportunities during the school day to practice listening, speaking, reading, and writing in English.

OTHER FACTORS

As is the case with non-ELs, individual circumstances can provide teachers with meaningful clues to a student's instructional needs. Teachers are encouraged to adopt a respectfully inquisitive perspective in order to glean as much information about student backgrounds as possible (e.g., interview parents, make home visits).

STUDENT INTERESTS

Knowledge about students' interests outside of school can be leveraged to enhance engagement and motivation in the classroom. For example, Vincente's creative teacher might capitalize on his soccer interest by setting up a reward system in which he can earn soccer-related items (e.g., a soccer jersey donated by a local sporting goods store) by demonstrating good behavior in class; a writing project might be personalized to report on a national soccer event, team, or player that will serve to motivate Vincente. Jessica's love of science must be recognized and supported in science classes that emphasize the development of the academic language associated with that discipline.

Table 2.1 reveals considerable variability among background characteristics for even a small group of ELs. Such variability increases exponentially with the addition of more students with different background characteristics.

Table 2.1 Differing Background Characteristics Across Example English Learners

	Chandra	Vincente	Marco	Jessica
Age	9	12	15	15
Grade	Third	Seventh	Ninth	Ninth
Family Background	Mother, father, maternal grandparents, aunt and uncle with three cousins	Came to United States. with single uncle, elderly grandmother, aunt and uncle with two cousins	Two parents (both bilingual), older brother attending Princeton, three-year-old sister	Two parents (neither speak English), two brothers and two sisters
Country of Origin/ Country of Domicile	Nepal	Mexico	Brazil	United States
Immigrant/ Refugee/ Migrant/ Other Status	Bhutanese refugee (born in refugee camp in Nepal)	Immigrant	Immigrant	US Citizen
Living Situation (e.g., housing, homelessness)	Crowded, run-down apartment in a declining neighborhood	Small house in a neighborhood inhabited entirely by Mexican and Central American immigrants	Palatial house in wealthy suburb	Apartment in a complex filled with Spanish-speaking residents

	Chandra	Vincente	Marco	Jessica
Socio-economic Status (e.g., food security)	Low socio-economic status, despite supporting each other by pooling resources	Middle socio-economic status, supporting each other by pooling resources	High socio-economic status	Low socio-economic status
Cultural Background/ Practices	Collectivistic culture that is distant from classmates, Hindu religion (with caste system and abstinence from beef, defined gender roles)	Collectivistic	Individualistic, competitive attitude; prefers to separate himself from the less advantaged	Collectivistic (in keeping with her parents' culture)
Educational Backgrounds / Content Knowledge, Skills, and Abilities	Attended refugee camp school (conducted in English)	Missed three years of school in Mexico (as reported by his uncle)	On grade level in Brazil (top of his class)	Attended US schools since kindergarten
First Language/ Script	Nepali/ Devanagari	Spanish, Roman script	Portuguese, Roman script	Spanish, Roman script
First Language Listening/ Speaking Levels	Assumed to be "fine" in social language; no academic language, as the school was English-medium (rather than Nepali) (no intake assessment in the first language)	Social language appropriate for a seventh grader in Spanish; academic language is well below grade level (determined by intake assessment in Spanish)	Father reports that he was at the top of his class; the family provided supporting transcripts (no intake assessment in the first language)	Strong social language, minimal academic language skills
First Language Reading/ Writing Levels	Limited—parents taught her; no assessment available (asked parents for details but no interpreter available)	Second grade (determined by intake assessment in Spanish)	Grade level (according to parents)	Minimal
Length of Time in the United States	1 year	1 month	6 months	15 years

(Continued)

Table 2.1 (Continued)

	Chandra	Vincente	Marco	Jessica
English Listening/ Speaking Levels	Level 3 in both (came at Level 3) —attended school sporadically in English in the camp	Level 1 in both	Level 4 in both	Level 4 in both
English Reading/ Writing Levels	Level 2 in reading (came at Level 2), Level 1 in writing— attended school sporadically in English in the camp	Level 1 in both	Level 4 in both (private tutors in Brazil)	Level 3 in both
Exposure to English Outside of School	TV only, other kids in the apartment complex	TV only, enclave community where English is not needed	Parents are bilingual, social interactions within the community and in the home (family speaks English on even calendar days)	Communication with school friends, Spanish spoken in the home
Other factors (e.g., gifted/ talented, special education, physical disabilities)	Teachers want to refer her for special education, as she is "significantly discrepant" from peers; lack of interpreter/ translator has stalled this process	Just wants to go back to Mexico; lacking motivation to learn English, as he can speak Spanish at home (and even at school); totally disengaged from school; has been taken to the principal for fighting in the cafeteria and throwing a chair	Identified as gifted (due to pressure from parents); his vision is defined by his parents' goals; he plans to attend an Ivy League school in the United States (as his father did and his brother is doing)	Long-term English learner, stuck in remedial courses that do not advance her academic language in ways that are necessary to her exit from English language development programming
Student Interests	She enjoys nature and engages in drawing when supplies are available.	His love for soccer and the opportunity to play in his neighborhood motivate him.	He enjoys practicing the cello, with a significant goal in mind: playing in the symphony.	Would like to become a nurse, loves science.

This wealth of information composed of student background characteristics constitutes essential and robust data that must inform and drive the instruction and assessment of ELs. Since many data resulting from traditional tests lack accuracy (Fairbairn & Fox, 2009), school-based teams must make use of accessible data that are truly meaningful, such as the student background characteristics described above. Administrators and teachers must work against the tendency to "attend systematically to certain data and to systematically avoid or ignore other data" (Wagner et al., 2006, p. 175). Instead, they must make use of relevant EL-specific data that truly represent the knowledge, skills, and abilities of those students and inform stakeholders of the realities that these students face. A clear understanding of these realities, particularly when ELs are known personally, will empower teachers and administrators with the collective will to effectively serve these students.

Returning to the abacus analogy, each student's individual characteristics dictate the response from school-based teams. The team-based approach will ensure that the best interests and long-range goals of ELs can be met, based on the will to do so, grounded in a shared vision.

Gain Input From Each Relevant Stakeholder Group

In order to understand the current EL reality within a given district or school, EL parent and student voices must be heard and integrated, along with those of knowledgeable individuals who work with these parents and students. First-person voices must be incorporated at every possible opportunity if the shared vision is to be truly inclusive and responsive to ELs and parents. Necessary interpretation/translation into the languages best understood by parents must be available to support such involvement. Further, developing awareness and understanding of cultural ways of communicating is an essential aspect of gaining first-person EL input; some cultural groups may hesitate to participate based on fear, lack of schema for school involvement, or even feeling unwelcome at the school. Those who do participate may communicate concerns indirectly or in an understated way or may not communicate them at all, due to cultural norms.

Step 2: Coconstruct "a clear statement of the desired outcomes ('what we want to create together')" (Senge et al., 2012, p. 88)

Whichever vision districts/schools claim to enact for all students must unequivocally encompass ELs, without exception. The development of the shared district/school vision for serving ELs provides the opportunity to articulate how the district/school specifically addresses ELs in its philosophy, programs, and services. Ensuring stakeholder involvement to coconstruct the statement of desired outcomes, in which ELs are explicitly included, is a prerequisite to implementation.

> Shared buy-in to the change effort is essential in achieving the goal of meeting the needs of ELLs campuswide. . . . Every teacher must become a leader in fostering a school culture that promotes students' language acquisition and furthers student learning. Ultimately, in successful school change effort, the values, beliefs, and norms of the educators must support the change for sustained practices and processes. Ultimately, in strengthening a school culture that supports high achievement for all ELLs, shared beliefs include the benefits of a second language, an appreciation of cultural differences, and the need to overcome stereotypes and inequities. (Alford & Niño, 2011, p. 3)

The process of synthesizing desired outcomes from each stakeholder group will culminate in producing the collective shared vision that explicitly ensures comprehensive inclusion of ELs.

Gain Input from Each Relevant Stakeholder Group

Each group of stakeholders, using their selected norms, will contribute a list of desired outcomes in terms of meeting EL needs. In addition to thoughtfully discussing how the district/school overarching vision statement can be tailored to fully integrate ELs and their families, another possible approach includes review and discussion of EL vision statements that have been created by other districts/schools, which are readily available online. These varied vision statements can serve as an excellent springboard for discussion and can broaden thinking. Stakeholder groups can then generate lists of desired outcomes that will enhance the current EL reality.

Categorize and Prioritize Ideas About Desired Outcomes

Each stakeholder group then categorizes and priorities its list of desired outcomes. Suggested categories might include, but not be limited to, the following:

- Literacy development, particularly for those preliterate in the L1
- Academic achievement
- Family literacy

- Parent involvement
- Extracurricular activity inclusion
- Inclusion in gifted/talented and all other programs
- Supports for newcomer families
- Interpretation/translation
- Grading/report cards
- Postgraduation connections

In order to synthesize ideas from all stakeholder groups, the leadership team might collect all prioritized recommendations and dedicate their efforts to combining them.

Write the Vision Statement, Incorporating All Stakeholder Input

Once all stakeholder input has been condensed into a single working document, the lead team will work to finalize the vision statement. This process is likely to be time intensive; it is recommended that several work sessions be scheduled in order to accomplish the work.

Gather Public Comments

After the vision statement has been crafted by the lead team, it is ready for public comment. Districts/schools may elect to seek only stakeholder group input, or they may wish to seek input from a wider audience to enhance the statement.

Submit Vision Statement to Relevant Leaders for Approval

Each district/school will follow its own procedures for gaining approval of the new, shared, EL vision statement. This may require gaining approval from the principal, district office, and/or school board.

Step 3: Coconstruct "a collective choice about how to proceed" (Senge et al., 2012, p. 88)

Based on Finalized Vision Statement, Identify Potential Barriers to Success (Bainbridge, 2007)

Once board approval has been secured, the stakeholder groups reconvene to identify potential barriers to the success of their coconstructed vision. At this point, stakeholder groups may be reconfigured to address grade-level, subject-area, or building-specific concerns.

Determine Action Steps (Bainbridge, 2007)

For each potential barrier, stakeholder groups brainstorm action steps to enhance outcomes for ELs. This document will be useful for program review when the stakeholder groups evaluate the efficacy of their efforts (see Chapter 7).

COMMUNICATE THE FINAL VISION AND ACTION STEPS

The leadership team will determine how best to communicate the final EL vision statement and associated action steps. This may be done in a variety of ways (e.g., posting on the district website, presenting at grade-level meetings, presenting at a school board meeting). Publicizing, setting high expectations, and emphasizing leadership support for implementation of the shared EL vision will help to ensure that the collective efforts and time investment of all stakeholders are honored and operationalized.

SUPPORT STAKEHOLDERS IN ENACTING THE VISION

> When the fear of accountability overrides what is best for children and the attainment of both content and language, the principal must reevaluate his or her school's practice. . . . The principal, as leader, must show courage. This courage is founded on a conviction that doing what is right for children will inevitably show positive results. (Alford & Niño, 2011, p. 4)

While the term *accountability* has overtones of punishment or negative consequences, school leaders can focus on the positive aspects of embracing responsibility for ELs by emphasizing support available at the district/school level for enacting the shared EL vision. In this way, all stakeholders work toward the same goals and can honor and highlight the accomplishments of each other. One way for school leaders to support all stakeholders in the EL learning and assessment process is through consideration of how stakeholders would answer the "Big Six" questions developed by Knight (2007, p. 206):

- Do I know what is expected of me?
- Do I have the materials and equipment I need to do my work right?
- At work, do I have the opportunity to do what I do best every day?
- In the past seven days, have I received recognition or praise for doing good work?

- Is there someone at work who cares about me?
- Is there someone at work who encourages my development?

School leaders must work to ensure that every school employee can answer all six questions with a resounding "Yes!" These questions set the stage for managing change in districts/schools. The resulting positive environment supports teachers in risk taking and innovation, which lead to the refinement of practices to meet the needs of ELs.

ACKNOWLEDGE, CELEBRATE, AND REWARD EFFORTS

In order to effectively manage change, Knight (2007) recommends that individuals be credited for their work on at least a weekly basis. School administrators and school board members should brainstorm ways to support, validate, and encourage all stakeholders for progress made in the implementation of the shared EL vision. These leaders can consult the action steps generated by stakeholder groups as a starting point for reviewing progress. A process of peer nomination for district/school recognition can be instituted, as well (see Template 2.1 at the end of this chapter).

RESOURCE 2.1 Developing a Vision Statement

Task	Person(s) Responsible	Action Steps	Timeline
Establish norms for lead team members			
Identify all appropriate stakeholders			
Plan the meeting schedule and location			
Convene stakeholders			
Establish norms for the group			
Enact the vision planning and writing process.			
• Coconstruct a clear picture of the current reality			
o Explore the heterogeneity of the students and their distinct EL background characteristics			
o Gain input from each relevant stakeholder group			
• Coconstruct a clear statement of the desired outcomes (what we want to create together)			
o Gain input from each relevant stakeholder group			
o Categorize and prioritize ideas about desired outcomes			
o Write the vision statement, incorporating all stakeholder input			
o Gather public comments			
o Submit to relevant leaders for final approval			
• Coconstruct a collective choice about how to proceed			
o Based on finalized vision statement, identify potential barriers to success			
o Determine action steps			
Communicate the final vision and action steps			
Support stakeholders in enacting the vision			
Acknowledge, celebrate, and reward efforts			

TEMPLATE 2.1 Nomination Form

PEER NOMINATION for EL EXTRA EFFORT (E³) RECOGNITION	
Nominee (name and email): Position: Building:	Date: Submit to:
Nominated by (name and email): Building: Position:	
Description of activities focused on EL vision implementation:	

Name and Capitalize Upon Relevant Expertise Within Collaborative Teams

3

The research has been clear and consistent for over 30 years—collaborative cultures in which teachers focus on improving their teaching practice, learn from each other, and are well led and supported by school principals result in better learning for students.

(Fullan, 2011b, p. 2)

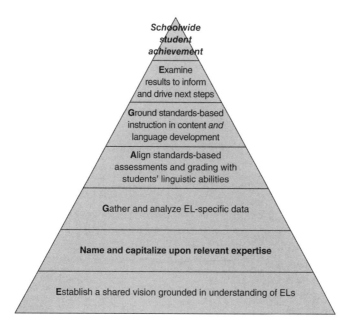

WHY SHARE EXPERTISE?

In an age of burgeoning EL demographics, increasingly rigorous student learning standards, and ever-tightening budgets, district-/school-based teams must identify and engage the full range of their collective expertise in order to facilitate student achievement. Educators must feel free to access the wide array of expertise and resources of their colleagues in order to expand their own capacity to meet the needs of ELs. Initiating the second step of the ENGAGE model (naming and capitalizing upon relevant expertise) is essential to ensuring that those needs are met.

THE PROCESS OF BUILDING CAPACITY

To build educator capacity, school leaders must initiate and facilitate the following five-step process in their contexts:

1. Convene relevant stakeholders (e.g., a building- or grade-level team, a professional learning community (PLC).

2. Share areas of expertise and resources.

3. Determine how to creatively capitalize upon all represented expertise and resources to increase EL achievement.

4. Establish ongoing mechanisms for communication and collaboration.

5. Recognize and celebrate successes.

Figure 3.1 illustrates three potential ways to carry out this capacity-building process of naming and capitalizing upon expertise, which will widely vary across schools and districts.

Convene Relevant Stakeholders

Having convened diverse groups of representatives, each facilitator team supports the group members in identifying the skills and resources that they each possess that could be applicable to facilitating EL services, ultimately increasing student academic achievement.

Share Relevant Areas of Expertise and Resources

Each school team chose different ways of sharing relevant cultural and linguistic expertise, and resources (*italicized*), revealing a wealth of contributions (see Figure 3.2).

Figure 3.1 Example Stakeholder Teams

Mountain View Community School District serves 995 students at one elementary school, one middle school, and one high school. Because a meat packing plant has recently located in their town, the community has experienced an influx of immigrant and refugee families from Mexico, Honduras, El Salvador, Sudan, and Burma who speak a variety of languages. The superintendent, who had been concerned about declining enrollment, recognizes that the increased EL enrollment in the school district serves as both a blessing and a challenge. Classrooms are filled to capacity once again, but teachers are struggling to appropriately engage their new students in the curriculum.

As a result, this superintendent and her leadership team plan to conduct meetings in each of their schools to determine the strengths and resources that school employees bring to the table. The superintendent elects to empower leadership at each building to make decisions about how to carry out the process.

Sunrise Elementary School (The principal convenes and facilitates a meeting of the entire staff with administrative support from a trusted teacher leader.)	**Brookview Middle School** (The principal designates the school counselor to be the lead facilitator of this work. He requests assistance from a teacher leader.)	**Foothills High School** (The principal tasks the two at-risk teachers to convene a team. These teachers elect to solicit volunteers.)
• ESL teacher (teacher leader) • Title I reading teacher • Title I math teacher • Grade-level teachers • G/T teacher • "Specials" teachers (art, music, PE) • Special education teachers • Paraeducators/ associates • Instructional coach (with ESL expertise)[1] • Counselor • Principal • Curriculum director • English learner parent representatives • Parent-Teacher Organization member	• Special education teacher (teacher leader) • Four language arts/ social studies teachers • Four math/science teachers • Special education paraeducator/ associate • ESL paraeducator/ associate (part time) • Instructional coach (with ESL expertise) • Counselor • Parent volunteers	• Two at-risk teachers (teacher leaders) • Two special education teachers • English teacher • Physical science teacher • Math teacher • PE teacher/coach • Instructional coach (with ESL expertise) • Student resource officer (SRO) • Counselor • A school board member • Civic organization representatives (e.g., one from the Lions Club and one from the Rotary Club) • (The team requests that the principal join later in the process.)

---

[1] In order to adequately support teachers of ELs, instructional coaches must possess expertise in how to effectively serve ELs. This expertise is absolutely essential to the coaching process and should be nonnegotiable when hiring.

Figure 3.2 Example Areas of Stakeholder Expertise and Resources

Sunrise Elementary School	Brookview Middle School	Foothills High School
Members of this group shared information in small group discussions and took notes on chart paper. Their work on this step culminated with a gallery walk to view the contributions of each individual.	Members of this group engaged in a t-chart activity, wherein each individual (see Figure 3.1 for a list of individuals) used sticky notes to list areas of expertise and resources. (Names were included on each note for later reference.)	Members of this group shared information via a spreadsheet posted and shared electronically. Large-group discussion of the identified information followed.
<ul><li>ESL teacher knows ESL strategies to scaffold learning for diverse students across all grade levels and subject areas, has sponsored refugees in resettlement process, has *multilingual books and picture dictionaries.*</li><li>Title I reading teacher also has a Spanish endorsement and *English-Spanish dictionaries.*</li><li>Title I math teacher also has a special education endorsement.</li><li>Grade-level teachers are experts in their grade-level content.<ul><li>*One teacher was born in Laos and was an EL herself.*</li><li>*Math teacher has manipulatives.*</li><li>*Reading teacher has leveled nonfiction books.*</li><li>*One teacher speaks Spanish fairly well.*</li><li>*One teacher served in the Peace Corps in Central America and has some cultural insights to share.*</li></ul></li><li>G/T teacher has expertise regarding ways to differentiate instruction and assessment across all grade levels and subject areas, has *books and artifacts from different countries.*</li></ul>	<ul><li>Special education teacher studied in Spain one semester, has *materials for students with lower reading levels, manipulatives and posters related to content areas, iPads.*</li><li>Four language arts/social studies teachers<ul><li>One hosted a foreign exchange student from Costa Rica, *has a collection of international flags.*</li><li>One attended several ESL-specific sessions at a national conference, learning some excellent strategies, *has several books focused on hands-on teaching strategies.*</li><li>One has a brother-in-law from Mexico, *willing to drive students to appointments, willing to help parents and older students find jobs.*</li><li>One attended a year-long sheltered instruction professional development initiative in her last school district, *has sheltered instruction resources and lesson plans.*</li></ul></li></ul>	<ul><li>Two at-risk teachers (teacher leaders)<ul><li>Both are skilled with a wide variety of instructional strategies, *have high-interest, lower reading-level books.*</li></ul></li><li>Two special education teachers<ul><li>One travels to Southeast Asia every summer.</li><li>One supports an orphan in the Philippines, *willing to take students to appointments.*</li></ul></li><li>English teacher is a former refugee from Bosnia, brings insight about learning English as a second language, *willing to teach students how to drive.*</li><li>Physical science teacher is on a soccer team in the state capital with mostly international teammates, *willing to transport others who might be interested in joining the soccer league.*</li><li>Math teacher is skilled at identifying students in need of college connections, application</li></ul>

Sunrise Elementary School	Brookview Middle School	Foothills High School

• "Specials" teachers (art, music, PE)
 	
  ○ Music teacher is interested in using music from students' countries of origin, *has instruments from different countries.*
  ○ Art teacher focuses on multicultural art in each unit of instruction *and has access to craft materials for special assignments.*
  ○ PE teacher is interested in teaching more international games/sports in her curriculum, *willing to start intramural sports teams for beginners.*
 	
• Special education teachers have worked with ELs in the past, *have curricular materials to support students at lower reading levels.*
• Paraeducators/ associates—one is bilingual in Spanish, one took Russian in college; *both are willing to work under the direction of a teacher to support ELs.*
• Counselor has an endorsement in French, *conducts staff development on multicultural backgrounds of students at the school.*
• Principal taught in a very diverse school for his first two years after college; *he and his wife sponsor a refugee family in town.*
• Curriculum director taught special education, *ensures that EL concerns are brought to the forefront in district meetings.*
	• Four math/science teachers
	
	  ○ One taught English in Africa (Chad) for two years during her Peace Corps service, *has artifacts and photos from Africa on display in her room.*
	  ○ One has a spouse who volunteers at the Hispanic Outreach Center in the state capital once per month, *willing to transport interested individuals to the center each month.*
	  ○ One participated in a mission trip to Haiti with his church.
	  ○ One took two years of Spanish in college, *willing to help with parent communication.*
	
	• Special education paraeducator/associate has an elementary reading endorsement, *willing to work with ELs with limited reading skill.*
	• ESL paraeducator/ associate (part-time) has supported students in Reading Recovery, develops rapport with students quickly.
	• Instructional coach (with ESL expertise) has the ESL endorsement, *willing to facilitate after-school girls' club, willing to raise funds for identified student needs.*
	• Counselor has a son-in-law from Cambodia, *willing to create a clothes closet for needy families.*
		completion, et cetera and *willing to assist them.*
		• PE teacher/coach is *willing to mentor students through sports.*
		• Instructional coach is former science teacher who emphasizes and models the use of demonstrations, visual aids, et cetera in her work with teachers.
		• School resource officer hosts an after-school boys' group, *provides a strong male role model.*
		• Counselor took a course in cross-cultural counseling, *willing to start an ESL parents' group for K–12 parents.*
		• A school board member is influential in local organizations that support and fund school activities, *willing to advocate in the community for ELs and their families.*
		• Civic organization representatives (i.e., one from the Lions Club and one from the Rotary Club) have connections with optical health care providers and are *willing to fund optical health care for students in need, willing to collect/ fund musical instruments for students interested in band.*
		• Principal *greets students each morning in their first languages and pronounces their names correctly.*
		• School secretary *places an emphasis on pronouncing student names accurately.*

(Continued)

Figure 3.2 (Continued)

Sunrise Elementary School	Brookview Middle School	Foothills High School
• English learner parent representatives have bilingual skills, intercultural skills, *knowledge about their previous education system, understanding of culture shock*. • Parent–Teacher Organization member has *connections to monetary resources*. • Custodians *help to provide a welcoming environment by verbal interaction with students*.	• Parent volunteer adopted a child from Russia, *willing to provide child care for immigrant/refugee families, willing to collect furniture for needy families*. • Food service workers *ensure that food choices are respectful of student religious preferences and are labeled appropriately; greet students when they arrive in the cafeteria by learning words in their languages*.	school announcements, focuses on positive interactions when ELs arrive late or need her assistance, goes out of her way to be welcoming to parents who come to the school office to deliver a forgotten lunch or assignment to an EL. • Bus drivers *pronounce student names correctly, greet students in their languages*.

The aforementioned examples of relevant cultural and linguistic expertise and resources represent a small sampling. Educators are encouraged to think outside of the box in terms of the skills and resources that they possess that could be useful in supporting ELs. Once these skills and resources have been identified and shared, the next step is to determine how to best use them to support student success.

Determine How to Creatively Capitalize Upon All Represented Expertise and Resources to Increase EL Achievement

Drawing from information in Figure 3.2, Figure 3.3 illustrates how three different educators with varying areas of expertise and resources to offer could apply them, maximizing support for ELs. These examples are meant to expand thinking about how any and all educators can use their strengths to support and encourage ELs in their contexts.

Since ELs represent the fastest-growing demographic group nationally, many teachers without credentials in ESL, bilingual education, or dual language instruction have these students in their classes. With or without a specific credential, all teachers as well as other school staff possess skills, talents, and strengths. When viewed through an EL Lens, these attributes can be accessed in meaningful and creative ways on behalf of ELs to promote a safe and welcoming environment.

Based in our own practice, following are additional ideas that operationalize the expertise and resources for the benefit of EL academic

Figure 3.3 Examples of Application of Expertise and Resources

Sunrise Elementary School	Brookview Middle School	Foothills High School
The PE teacher was interested in teaching more international games/sports in her curriculum and *willing to start intramural sports teams for beginners.* Based on these strengths, this teacher enabled inexperienced ELs to build background about teamwork, sportsmanship, and relationships through starting an intramural basketball program. She enlisted the help of the ESL teacher in communicating with ELs and their parents about the new opportunity. The Parent–Teacher Organization member spearheaded the design and purchase of team t-shirts and other equipment for the team. In addition, she called upon other parents (both EL and non-EL) to assist with driving and the provision of snacks after practice. These collaborative efforts resulted in improved behavior and academic achievement. The students were eventually able to compete with other intramural teams in the area.	One language arts/social studies teacher attended a year-long sheltered instruction professional development initiative in her last school district and *has sheltered instruction resources and lesson plans in his files.* This teacher volunteered to mentor other interested teachers in a series of before-school discussions. She asked the special education teacher and a math/science teacher to join forces with her in this endeavor. The language arts/social studies teacher shared information about the components of sheltered instruction at each session, along with example resources and lesson plans. The special education teacher demonstrated iPad apps for each of the components, while the math/science teacher shared ways to incorporate sheltered instruction into those content areas. In follow-up sessions, the lead teacher coached others in preparing their own sheltered instruction lesson plans. Thanks to the instructional leadership of the principal, who supported the collaboration, these sessions took place during the school day.	The counselor had taken a course in cross-cultural counseling and *started an ESL parents' group for K–12 parents* that addressed topics generated by parents; group meetings included interpreters. The counselor researched components needed for a successful ESL parent group: • knowledge of parents' backgrounds and first languages • time and location that is convenient and accessible for participants • refreshments (donated) • child care (volunteers) • transportation (car pool or school bus) • personal invitations to parents (e.g., call home in the first language) • interpreters This teacher enlisted the help of the English teacher, with her insights into refugee experiences; the math teacher, with his college connections; and the school resource officer, with his commitment to serve as a male role model in the after-school boys' group. All four of these educators collaborated to carry out the successful first meeting. The initial parent meeting featured the local fire department describing fire safety and distributing free smoke detectors. At the end of the meeting, interpreters polled the participants regarding topics for future meetings.

achievement by addressing a range of opportunities and challenges. This list can be used as a springboard to generate additional ideas from your own context or as a way for school staff to select preferred activities and to identify teams. A template for this purpose is provided in Resource 3.1 at the end of the chapter.

- Seeking donations from local businesses (e.g., funds for medical needs, refreshments for diversity events)
- Partnering with local businesses to raise funds (e.g., cooking demo/ culture fair and gift wrapping at a bookstore, cooking demo at local gift shop)
- Assisting with making medical appointments for students
- Writing letters of recommendation to assist students in securing admission to college and associated scholarships
- Completing college/university and social services forms for families who need assistance
- Sharing cultural information and addressing US citizenship questions in school displays
- Giving ELs a voice in school newsletters (including student writing in those newsletters)
- Organizing school–community diversity events
- Incorporating international music into school concerts
- Facilitating student-to-student sharing of ELs' realities (e.g., student panels in classes)
- Conducting ESL summer school and evening ESL classes for adults
- Encouraging and supporting extracurricular activity participation
- Making and distributing multilingual birthday cards to school staff
- Planning and hosting graduation celebrations for ELs
- Organizing parent volunteers to assist ELs with homework (and organizing appreciation events for those volunteers)
- Creating artifacts to share with the community (e.g., international cookbook, collection of immigration stories written by ESL students)
- Assisting libraries to acquire multilingual and multicultural books
- Supporting ELs to prepare and deliver school board presentations
- Writing articles for the local newspaper about EL accomplishments
- Hosting communitywide appreciation events
- Engaging ELs in volunteer opportunities (e.g., refugee sponsorship)
- Encouraging and supporting ELs' competition in essay contests (local, state, and/or national)

- Empowering ELs to be ambassadors in other school districts, in the media, at conferences, et cetera
- Partnering with community and civic organizations (e.g., United Methodist Women, Veterans of Foreign Wars) to share cultural insights via presentations, guest participation at local political events, et cetera
- Assisting with preparation, application, and payment for the US Citizenship Test
- Working with interpreters in order to ensure that parents and students understand school policies
- Facilitating field trips to community places of interest (e.g., state capitol, historical museum, civic center, botanical center, TV station, college campuses)
- Creating and providing professional development and associated resources for educators
- Ensuring parent participation at parent–teacher conferences by communicating in advance with parents in their languages and providing interpreters at conferences
- Honoring US military members through "Valentines for Veterans" and Happy New Year letters to overseas military personnel from ELs
- Consulting with other school districts about how to best serve ELs
- Coordinating with college/university ESL student teaching programs
- Preparing and delivering teacher in-service sessions on EL topics
- Recognizing and honoring colleagues publically for achievements in serving ELs
- Collaborating with colleges/universities to give ELs an opportunity to share their experiences with future teachers
- Raising funds to support others (e.g., Red Cross, US Citizenship Test application fee, donation to family after death of a parent, Make-a-Wish Foundation, America's Fund for Afghan Children)
- Providing multicultural/ESL in-service for new staff
- Facilitating finding pen pals with ELs in other parts of the country or internationally
- Collecting and sharing holiday gifts for needy families
- Enacting simulations to increase awareness of EL realities (e.g., language immersion experiences)

Having committed to various activities based on identified individual areas of expertise and resources, stakeholders must ensure that information is shared with the wider community.

Establish Ongoing Mechanisms for Communication and Collaboration

There are a variety of ways that teams can disseminate information about individual stakeholder strengths and activities that have been undertaken based on those strengths. Examples of how to maintain a cycle of ongoing communication and improvement in meeting EL needs are described in Figure 3.4.

Constructing a supportive environment where ELs can thrive and academic achievement can soar requires the collective will of the entire district-/school-based team. Such comprehensive activities taking place in the district/school constitute newsworthy information; all stakeholders in the EL educational process must be made aware of these efforts, both within and outside of each building. As such, dedicated school staff should not hesitate to publicize their successes for district-/school-wide general knowledge. Highlighting the contributions, successes will instill pride and contribute to an overall positive morale.

Recognize and Celebrate Successes

A motivating mantra in our practice has been, "It doesn't have to be drudgery." Encouraging students to adopt an attitude of gratitude and focusing on student and staff contributions is key to enacting a vision for

Figure 3.4 Example Mechanisms for Communication and Collaboration

Sunrise Elementary School	Brookview Middle School	Foothills High School
The elementary school team determined that they would conduct biweekly meetings to update each other on current progress, successes, and challenges. This information was shared orally with the entire staff in the meetings and on an "EL Highlights" bulletin board in the staff lounge.	The middle school team met monthly to share accomplishments and brainstorm solutions. Information was recorded by a designated scribe and shared with the entire staff electronically. In addition, the team created a listserv for sharing new EL strategies and resources with each other on an ongoing basis.	The high school team conducted quarterly meetings. Subgroups who collaborated on individual activities such as the parent meetings described in Figure 3.3 met on an as-needed basis. Information was shared electronically with the entire staff and submitted to the superintendent's office for distribution in the *Superintendent's Communiqué.*

meeting the needs of ELs. There are many ways to carry out these well-deserved celebrations; three examples are shown in Figure 3.5.

Celebrating success is closely tied to enacting the district-/school-wide vision. When educators unite through a mutually adopted understanding of what must take place every day for English learners and feel that they can personally make a difference, they are spurred to greater heights. New collaborative relationships form in schools and districts, limited only by the participants' imagination of how they can bring their expertise and resources to bear. As these relationships solidify and grow, momentum and the will to refine and expand practice on behalf of ELs also increase. Further ensuring the proliferation of relationships, school-based celebrations that honor accomplishments reinforce a collegial and team-oriented collective will to carry out the vision and continue the work. Further, such a positive environment contributes to a general spirit of camaraderie and collegiality where overall morale can flourish.

Figure 3.5 Example Celebrations of Success

Sunrise Elementary School	Brookview Middle School	Foothills High School
The students on the intramural basketball team asked the ESL teacher to help them thank the adults who supported their team at the end-of-year school assembly. They collaboratively designed and signed a poster for each adult expressing their gratitude. The team cocaptains each gave a speech, and refreshments, which had been donated by a local grocery store, were served afterward.	The middle school principal nominated the sheltered instruction professional development team for the Chamber of Commerce annual "Best Teacher" award. After a short deliberation, chamber members determined that granting awards to all team members was appropriate. The teachers attended an evening banquet, and each received an engraved plaque and mention in the local newspaper.	The Mountain View School Board invited the EL parent organization participants to their end-of-year meeting. While the parents initially expected the usual meeting to take place, they were surprised when they were each honored for their participation in this new initiative and their contributions to the school district. Each parent received a certificate of appreciation and an activity pass for all school events the following year.

RESOURCE 3.1 Template for the Process of Naming and Capitalizing on Relevant Expertise Within Collaborative Teams

Linguistic/Cultural Expertise and Resources	Names	How Expertise Will Be Capitalized Upon to Support EL Success	Timeline
Seeking donations from local businesses (e.g., funds for medical needs, refreshments for diversity events)			
Partnering with local businesses to raise funds (e.g., cooking demo/culture fair and gift wrapping at a bookstore, cooking demo at local gift shop)			
Assisting with making medical appointments for students			
Writing letters of recommendation to assist students in securing admission to college and associated scholarships			
Completing college/university and social services forms for families who need assistance			
Sharing cultural information and US citizenship questions in school displays			
Giving ELs a voice in school newsletters (including student writing in those newsletters)			
Organizing school–community diversity events			
Incorporating international music into school concerts			
Facilitating student-to-student sharing of ELs' realities (e.g., student panels in classes)			
Conducting ESL summer school and evening ESL classes for adults			
Encouraging and supporting extracurricular activity participation			

Linguistic/Cultural Expertise and Resources	Names	How Expertise Will Be Capitalized Upon to Support EL Success	Timeline
Making multilingual birthday cards for school staff and distributing them			
Planning and hosting graduation celebrations for ELs			
Organizing parent volunteers to assist ELs with homework (and organizing appreciation events for those volunteers)			
Creating artifacts to share with the community (e.g., international cookbook, collection of immigration stories written by ESL students)			
Assisting libraries to acquire multilingual and multicultural books			
Supporting ELs in preparing and delivering school board presentations			
Writing articles for the local newspaper about EL accomplishments			
Hosting communitywide appreciation events			
Engaging ELs in volunteer opportunities (e.g., refugee sponsorship)			
Encouraging and supporting ELs' competition in essay contests (local, state, and/or national)			
Empowering ELs to be ambassadors in other school districts, in the media, at conferences, et cetera			
Partnering with community and civic organizations (e.g., United Methodist Women, Veterans of Foreign Wars) to share cultural insights via presentations, guest participation at local political events, etc.			

(Continued)

RESOURCE 3.1 (Continued)

Linguistic/Cultural Expertise and Resources	Names	How Expertise Will Be Capitalized Upon to Support EL Success	Timeline
Assisting with preparation, application, and payment for the US Citizenship Test			
Working with interpreters in order to ensure that parents and students understand school policies			
Facilitating field trips to community places of interest (e.g., state capitol, historical museum, civic center, botanical center, TV station, college campuses)			
Creating and providing professional development and associated resources for educators			
Ensuring parent participation at parent–teacher conferences by communicating in advance with parents in their languages and providing interpreters at conferences			
Honoring US military members through "Valentines for Veterans" and Happy New Year letters to overseas military personnel from ELs			
Consulting with other school districts about how to best serve ELs			
Coordinating with college/ university ESL student teaching programs			
Preparing and delivering teacher in-service sessions on EL topics			
Recognizing and honoring colleagues publicly for achievements in serving ELs			
Collaborating with colleges/ universities to provide ELs with opportunities to share their experiences with future teachers			

Linguistic/Cultural Expertise and Resources	Names	How Expertise Will Be Capitalized Upon to Support EL Success	Timeline
Raising funds to support others (e.g., Red Cross, US Citizenship Test application fee, donation to family after death of a parent, Make-a-Wish Foundation, America's Fund for Afghan Children)			
Providing multicultural/ESL in-service for new staff			
Facilitating finding pen pals with ELs in other parts of the country or internationally			
Collecting and sharing holiday gifts for needy families			
Enacting simulations to increase awareness of EL realities (e.g., language immersion experiences)			

Gather and Analyze EL-Specific Data

4

A variety of current educational initiatives claim their efforts target 'all' learners. However, without applying critical language acquisition principles and research, such generalized initiatives for all learners are destined to fall short in meeting the needs of ELLs. Research that claims to be useful for increasing ELL achievement should be considered for implementation with ELLs only if it has actually included these students and been interpreted from an ELL perspective. Administrators and teachers must interrogate both research and practice to ensure that they are truly meaningful for and applicable to ELLs, not simply generalized best practice.

(Jones-Vo & Fairbairn, 2012, ¶2)

By this point in your work to engage ELs in learning language and content, you have established a shared vision for serving ELs and named the expertise to capitalize upon within collaborative teams. It is now time to gather and analyze EL-specific data. When gathering and analyzing these data, the focus must be on gaining *accurate* understanding of what students know and can do independent of obstacles presented by the English language. Many sources of data that are available for ELs can underestimate their knowledge, skills, and abilities due to the confounding of English language ability with the *construct of interest* (what is really being assessed). As Menken (2000) asserts, "A test in English is a test *of* English." This chapter aims to assist teachers, administrators, and other relevant stakeholders in the process of accurately understanding what ELs know and can do by interpreting data through an EL Lens.

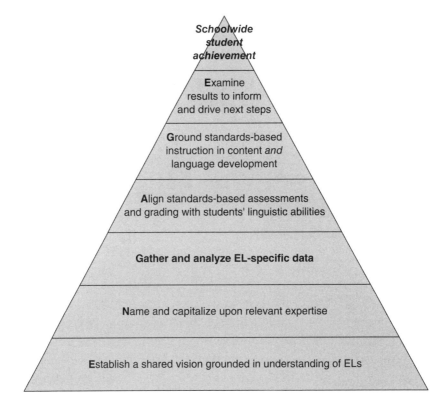

AREAS OF RESPONSIBILITY/ACTION FOR GATHERING AND ANALYZING EL-SPECIFIC DATA

Table 4.1 summarizes the stages in a district-/school-wide effort to gather and analyze EL-specific data for three key groups: leadership teams (composed of administrators and other school leaders), teachers, and other stakeholders (e.g., school board members, parents). Each area is described in detail in the sections that follow.

Stages 1–10 constitute the process of gathering and analyzing EL-specific data that will drive instruction and assessment, while stages 11 and 12 compose the teaching and assessment process outlined in later chapters. Stage 13 represents the recursive nature of the use of data to drive instruction.

Stage 1: Shared Understanding of ELs

Leadership Team Responsibilities/Actions

Although the coconstruction of shared understanding occurs initially during the development of the district-/school-wide vision, administrators bear the ongoing responsibility for ensuring that this shared understanding

Table 4.1 Areas of Responsibility/Action for Gathering and Analyzing EL-Specific Data

Stages/Areas of Responsibility	Leadership Team Responsibilities/Actions	Teacher Responsibilities/Actions	Other Stakeholder Responsibilities/Actions
1. Shared understanding of ELs	Build shared understanding of the backgrounds and needs of ELs on an ongoing basis (grounded in the visioning process described in Chapter 2)	Develop shared understanding of the backgrounds and needs of ELs on an ongoing basis (grounded in the visioning process described in Chapter 2)	Develop shared understanding of the backgrounds and needs of ELs on an ongoing basis (grounded in the visioning process described in Chapter 2)
2. Stakeholder involvement	Convene all relevant stakeholders for data analysis, being sure to include bilingual paraeducators/associates (include noncertified personnel such as food service, custodial, transportation, and office staff, as appropriate)	Participate in data teams to gather and analyze/interpret data	Participate in data teams to gather and analyze/interpret data
3. Infusion of an EL Lens in data analysis	Advocate for accurate EL data analysis at the district level and beyond (e.g., recognizing limitations of assessment data that do not take into account the complexity of ELs)	Incorporate insights related to the teaching and assessment of ELs	Actively communicate perspectives from diverse areas of expertise that enrich the interpretation of data *and* impact data-based decisions for ELs
4. Access to EL data	Ensure that every teacher has access to English language development test data	Seek out and utilize data to inform practice	Support the use of EL-specific data to inform practice
5. Collection of additional data, as needed	Value additional relevant EL data and support its collection	Know their ELs by collecting additional relevant data	Support efforts to collect additional relevant data
6. Honoring practitioner expertise	Respect and incorporate the insights of all educators (including pareducators/ associates and family advocates/liaisons) who are well versed in issues of linguistic and cultural	Willingly share insights related to the teaching and assessment of ELs	Support the sharing and incorporation of insights from all relevant individuals who are well versed in issues of linguistic and cultural diversity

(Continued)

Table 4.1 (Continued)

Stages/Areas of Responsibility	Leadership Team Responsibilities/Actions	Teacher Responsibilities/Actions	Other Stakeholder Responsibilities/Actions
	diversity; include food service, custodial, transportation, and office staff in this process, as appropriate		
7. Professional development	Seek out and provide EL-specific research-based PD for teachers and other relevant stakeholders (e.g., counselors, curriculum directors) in the appropriate analysis and interpretation of EL data	Participate in EL-specific research-based PD in the appropriate analysis and interpretation of EL data	Participate in EL-specific research-based PD in the appropriate analysis and interpretation of EL data
8. Data interpretation	Facilitate opportunities for analyzing and interpreting EL data	Collaborate with colleagues to accurately analyze and interpret EL data	Participate in the analysis and interpretation of EL data, as appropriate
9. Data-driven action	Set high expectations for implementing responsive instruction and assessment (e.g., through walk-through templates aligned with expectations); align expectations for all noncertified school staff	Apply analysis to collaboratively implement EL-appropriate teaching and assessment	Ensure that connections are made between data interpretation and existing services, revising as needed
10. Ongoing support	Make resources available to staff, embed needed planning/collaboration time into the school day, ensure the engagement of all district/school employees	Collaborate with teachers and other stakeholders to implement and refine practices	Support teachers and administrators through district/school budgetary decision making and allocations that support the equitable engagement of ELs
11. Feedback	Provide formative feedback to teachers and other staff (e.g., by using walk-through templates aligned with expectations)	Incorporate feedback from district administrators	Host stakeholders to provide progress updates
12. Sharing/publication of progress	Share the implementation process with relevant stakeholders (e.g., school board, community members, educators, parents, district/school staff)		
13. Next steps	Clarify next steps in the cycle of continuous improvement		

is continually revisited and updated. Throughout any given school year, the demographics of the ELs served by the district/school are likely to shift, signaling a need for the collection and analysis of new data; changes related to new stakeholder needs must be continually factored into district-/school-wide practice as a matter of course. As instructional leaders, administrators must cultivate the collective will to serve ELs as if the ELs were their own children. Based on their careful development and insistence on a welcoming, inclusive, and caring school culture, the members of leadership teams have the power to impact and inspire teacher motivation and practice to creative new levels. More essential to educators and stakeholders than implementing new instructional practices is establishing the foundational bedrock composed of a consistent district/school culture that values and supports ELs across grades, curricula, and buildings. Leadership team members must work to soften resistant attitudes and motivate more effective practices among certain less enthusiastic staff members. These team members must lead the way by personally advocating for and connecting with ELs and their families. By their example, leadership team members support the creation of a positive culture for ELs and pave the way to their increased achievement.

One high school principal in the authors' practice started each day in the ESL classroom of newly arrived refugees and ELs, where he encouraged, joked with, and developed relationships with the students. His friendly example, which validated the students and made them feel a welcome part of the school, influenced a transformation among apathetic and unwelcoming staff members. This administrator led the way for each staff member to welcome and celebrate new diversity and to find creative ways to engage ELs in all aspects of school life. Over time, the administrative attitude and high expectations for ELs infiltrated buildings across the district. Led by administrator example and consistent setting of high expectations for ELs, this district eventually won a statewide award for the success of its K–12 ESL program.

Teacher Responsibilities/Actions

In response to demographic shifts, teachers must actively do their part to become acquainted with the cultures, languages, and other background characteristics of the ELs in their classrooms. A sense of curiosity and respectful discovery can lead to participation in cultural events, community festivals, family milestone participation, and other multicultural celebrations and observances that support ELs and their families while making personal connections in the school and community. Personal insights gleaned from relationships with new students and their families must be shared widely, incorporated into classroom learning and activities, and recognized as contributing to the overall positive school culture. Such personal connections and experiences lead to enhanced motivation for engaging ELs in all aspects of school life. Rather than being motivated by punitive measures, Supreme Court decisions, federal or state statutes, or other measures, teachers grounded in the shared district/school philosophy and vision outperform those who simply comply. They tap into their instructional creativity and advocacy out of a sense of a caring relationship with their students. Such supportive self-selected dispositions of teachers demonstrate the epitome of an ideal district/school foundation conducive to EL achievement.

Other Stakeholder Responsibilities/Actions

This stakeholder group can be constituted of a variety of individuals. Community leaders must work to hone their awareness of demographic shifts and insist on inclusive representation of school board members, community members, paraeducators, school staff, and others in district/school initiatives, including the very group that is doing the work of gathering and analyzing EL-specific data. A collective awareness of the contributions made by newcomers to the community and by EL student successes, as well as a knowledge of the needs of the diverse community, must inform stakeholder decision making and policies. Aligned with administrators, other stakeholders support the "cultivation of the collective will" in their various contexts to approach ELs based on their shared, co-constructed philosophy.

Stage 2: Stakeholder Involvement

Leadership Team Responsibilities/Actions

Leadership team members must ensure that teachers and other stakeholders are involved in the data gathering and analysis process. While teachers can be expected to attend required data team meetings, with teams organized in a variety of appropriate configurations, bilingual paraeducators/associates must be included, and other relevant stakeholders (e.g., food service, custodial, transportation, and office staff) may actively participate in some or all of these data meetings as well. Alternatively, due to their conviction about the importance of advocating for ELs, leadership team members must support creative data collection and analysis in other ways (e.g., an administrator attends a meeting of a community organization [e.g., Lions Club, service clubs] to collect nontraditional data in the form of input, perspective, and support). District/school leaders are encouraged to think creatively in the quest to gather and interpret all meaningful EL data.

Teacher Responsibilities/Actions

Teachers are urged to embrace the critical importance of applying appropriate data to EL instruction and assessment. Further, their full and undistracted participation is essential at this early foundational stage in order to ultimately support and enhance the achievement of English learners.

Other Stakeholder Responsibilities/Actions

In full consideration of a district-/school-wide approach to increasing student achievement, the voices of all other stakeholders must be sought and incorporated. Including input from all stakeholders at this initial phase ensures the inclusion of nontraditional data that they alone can provide (e.g., bilingual paraeducator input about schooling norms in other countries, parental insights about aspirations for their children, food service personnel contributions related to dietary practices in various countries).

Stage 3: Infusion of an EL Lens in Data Analysis

Leadership Team Responsibilities/Actions

Informed leadership team members know that data interpretation focused on large-scale test data is often inaccurate and especially inadequate for application to ELs. They must work to support teachers and other stakeholders in interrogating the data from such tests for its accuracy and meaning. Further, these leaders must incorporate other sources of information that can better illuminate ELs' current levels of knowledge, skills, and abilities and their instructional needs, particularly as they differ from those of native speakers of English. Developing such an EL Lens requires

1. Acknowledging that the accurate interpretation of EL data is likely to yield conclusions for ELs that are different from those for native speakers of English

2. Interrogating the tests themselves—do they result in accurate data?
   a. Test in English is a test *of* English
      i. Test language
      ii. Accommodations aren't always that effective!
   b. Use of unfamiliar formats (T/F)
   c. Cultural bias
   d. What are we trying to assess? Why not use picture support?

    e. What does the research say about "indicators" (e.g., fluency assessment to determine reading difficulties)

    f. Translation of tests is problematic

3. Addressing norm group issues—normative data from large-scale tests aren't always particularly helpful

4. Understanding peer group comparisons—who is the "true" peer group?

5. Recognizing the need for additional data (e.g., background characteristics)

6. Combining all of this information to accurately make decisions about ELs' instruction and assessment

Each of these important aspects of accurately interpreting EL data is discussed below.

The starting point for this critical process is acknowledging that the accurate interpretation of EL data is likely to yield conclusions for ELs that are different from those for native speakers of English. Approaches used for analyzing non-EL data result in inaccurate understandings of what ELs know and can do, leading to inappropriate instructional and assessment practices (e.g., the overrepresentation of ELs in special education programming, the underrepresentation of ELs in gifted/talented programming). Analysis of EL data must take into account the linguistic and cultural realities of these students (e.g., student background characteristics discussed in Chapter 2). Further, it must be approached from a standpoint of an additive view of these students, rather than a deficit view. This means that students are credited for their "funds of knowledge" (Moll, 1992): the wealth of knowledge, skills, abilities, and experiences that they bring with them to school. This additive view assumes that there is "nothing wrong with" ELs (Ross, 2014), that they are ready to engage in meaningful learning and to achieve academically.

Given the acknowledgement that traditional interpretation of test data is likely to be inaccurate for ELs, what should educators do in order to interpret such data appropriately? The first step is to interrogate the tests themselves. Menken (2000) and others point out that a test *in* English is a test *of* English. For example, a science test written in English serves as an assessment of both science and English for ELs. Further, test language (e.g., "all of the following *except*") is identified as a distinct type of language (in addition to social and academic language) (Stevens, Butler, & Castellon-Wellington, 2000), which can itself act as a barrier for ELs in their attempts to demonstrate what they know and can do in the content areas. Cultural bias is yet another factor that can undermine the accuracy of large-scale testing of ELs (Abedi, 2009). Accommodations, often claimed to be a panacea for this issue, do not always level the playing field for ELs as intended (Kopriva, Emick, Hipolito-Delgado, & Cameron, 2007). An additional problem with the tests themselves as indicators of student achievement relates to the item formats. If students are unfamiliar with the format (e.g., multiple choice, true/false), these are unlikely to result in accurate data.

If the goal is to gain an understanding of what ELs know and can do, tests should be developed with this end in mind. It is widely recognized that bias in assessment tools is problematic (American Educational Research Association, American Psychological Association, & National Council on Measurement in Education, 1999) and results in inaccurate data. Visual support has been touted historically as an essential teaching practice to ensure that language does not obscure meaning (Omaggio, 1979), and visual support remains as best practice (e.g., Echevarria, Vogt, & Short, 2013).

For ELs, an absence of culturally and chronologically appropriate visual support (e.g., a cell phone rather than a rotary phone, a laptop rather than a typewriter) is yet another indicator of the problematic nature of many standardized achievement tests.

In a similar vein, the use of certain types of data to evaluate ELs' proficiency levels and estimate their instructional needs flies in the face of what educational research asserts. For example, fluency is often used as a measure of reading comprehension in early literacy assessments. While research illustrates the utility of this measure for non-ELs, research is equally clear about the fact that fluency does not necessarily serve as an accurate indicator of EL reading comprehension (e.g., Quirk & Beem, 2012). Such misapplied indicators result in inaccurate estimation of ELs' reading abilities and the misapplication of literacy instruction.

Well-meaning administrators may be tempted to request that assessments be translated for ELs in an effort to provide students an opportunity to demonstrate what they know and can do that is more comparable to what fluent speakers of English receive. However, this practice is fraught with problems (Solano-Flores, Trumbull, & Nelson-Barber, 2002). These researchers point out that culture and language are inextricably intertwined, and this precludes simple translation of tests. Further, student sensitivity to wording is not addressed through simple test translation. Finally, the language of the test must match the language of instruction, as it cannot be assumed that ELs are academically fluent in their first languages. For these reasons, tests should not be translated at the district/school level.

By understanding and sharing these facts with teachers, administrators will carry out an important part of their responsibility to ensure the appropriate analysis of EL-specific data.

Teacher Responsibilities/Actions

Teachers enrich the EL Lens used for data analysis by contributing their professional insights related to teaching and assessing ELs. They help to maintain a constant focus on the realities of ELs necessary to ensure the accurate analysis of data. Teachers familiar with ELs provide invaluable perspective on appropriate interpretation through the EL Lens. For example, while a non-ESL teacher might view the lack of transfer of learning from one lesson to the next as a possible indicator of the need for special education referral, a teacher familiar with the realities of ELs might suggest that the initial instruction was incomprehensible to the EL and therefore not transferrable (Hamayan, Marler, Sanchez-Lopez, & Damico, 2013). This sort of insight is essential if ELs' knowledge, skills, abilities, and instructional needs are to be accurately understood.

Other Stakeholder Responsibilities/Actions

Other stakeholders in the EL data gathering and analysis process (e.g., parents) can actively communicate their views, giving voice to important factors that might go otherwise unnoticed. For example, cultural differences in writing patterns and storytelling might influence the ways in which students respond to test prompts (Chamberlain, Guerra, & Garcia, 1999). These cultural realities may result in incorrect interpretation of students' answers, leaving their test scores inaccurate.

Stage 4: Access to EL Data

Leadership Team Responsibilities/Actions

In order to accurately interpret content test data, data teams must be apprised of each individual student's English language proficiency/development scores in a timely manner. Some districts/schools compile this information for teachers and provide it directly to teachers. Other districts/schools simply make all assessment data available to teachers online to inform their instruction. An essential key for leadership teams is to ensure that every teacher has access to all relevant data about her or his students in a user-friendly format.

Teacher Responsibilities/Actions

Teachers must take full advantage of the access to data provided to them by district/school administrators. Use of this requisite student information will empower them to positively impact EL academic achievement by focusing on the precise instructional leverage point to scaffold instruction and, correspondingly, to assess learning.

Other Stakeholder Responsibilities/Actions

The role of other stakeholders is to support the use of EL data to inform practice. These stakeholders can ask teachers about how data inform their day-to-day activities and promote more precise focus on ELs' needs.

Stage 5: Collection of Additional Data, as Needed

Leadership Team Responsibilities/Actions

While data from large-scale standardized achievement tests enjoys favored status for non-ELs, such data holds less importance for ELs, as previously stated. As a result, additional relevant data (e.g., student characteristics described in Chapter 2) take on greater significance. For example, knowledge about differences in the student's first language script (e.g., characters rather than letters or different print directionality) can better inform next instructional steps than can data from an achievement test. District/school leaders must give this type of nontest data its rightful place in district/school conversations about ELs. Further, they must support teachers in collecting this type of student-centered data. Such gathering of valuable nontest data may take the form of dedicated time for home visits, time during early dismissals to collate such data, or other ways that value both the teachers' efforts and the importance of the data.

Teacher Responsibilities/Actions

Teachers' effort to know their ELs is likely to include the collection of additional data about those students. Teachers are encouraged to be creative in their quest to understand ELs' motivations and interests as a means to enhance the data that can inform instruction and assessment.

Other Stakeholder Responsibilities/Actions

In their efforts to support the collection of additional data, stakeholders can provide ideas for the types of data to be collected and, in some cases, can provide such data themselves (e.g., parents can clarify cultural beliefs and customs). When stakeholders fully embrace the meaning of all data related to ELs, they are positioned to better promote supportive and inclusive district/school policies.

Stage 6: Honoring Practitioner Expertise

Leadership Team Responsibilities/Actions

Leadership team members need to understand and honor the role of paraeducators, particularly those who are bilingual, as these individuals play a pivotal role in the education of many ELs. Traditionally, the bilingual skills and cultural expertise of paraeducators are not adequately valued. Further, paraeducators may not be afforded the same level of respect as teachers (e.g., they may be referred to by their first names by teachers and students alike), despite doing very important work that calls upon them to be educational partners with the teacher. Finally, these essential educators are often paid very low wages. District/school leaders are urged to recognize and reward the contributions and insights of paraeducators as brokers of culture and language. In the same vein, the expertise and insights of teachers who work with ELs must be honored and incorporated into practice, including current and new district/school initiatives. Finally, leadership teams must also recognize the valuable contributions that can be made by food service, custodial, transportation, and office staff members.

Teacher Responsibilities/Actions

In an environment of administrative support, teachers must willingly share culturally and linguistically diverse insights and experiences that can inform appropriate analysis of EL-specific data. Keeping an ongoing awareness of ELs at the forefront of district/school conversations will support an accurate interpretation of data intended to describe ELs.

Other Stakeholder Responsibilities/Actions

Stakeholders play a critical role in supporting the sharing and incorporation of diverse perspectives from teachers, paraeducators, and others. While insisting that such perspectives be considered, stakeholders are also charged to contribute their own insights and diverse viewpoints.

Stage 7: Professional Development

Leadership Team Responsibilities/Actions

District/school leaders must both seek out and provide EL-specific research-based professional development opportunities addressing the appropriate analysis and interpretation of EL data through the EL Lens for teachers and other relevant stakeholders. Such professional development must clarify the differences between analyzing data for non-ELs and analyzing data by applying the EL Lens that is needed to arrive at accurate EL data analysis. Specific differences are outlined in Table 4.2. (Note that the EL interpretations are based upon real students from the authors' experiences.)

Teacher Responsibilities/Actions

Teachers must actively participate in professional development that focuses on the accurate analysis and interpretation of all data related to ELs. This requires that they continually ask questions from an EL perspective rooted in a belief that ELs are poised for success and ready to learn. Such an orientation positions teachers to take the role of student advocates throughout the analysis and interpretation of data and to equitably afford ELs access to the curriculum.

Other Stakeholder Responsibilities/Actions

Stakeholders, like teachers, must participate in research-based professional development workshops focused on the use of EL-specific data. These stakeholders, having adopted the role of EL advocate, can continue to push the thinking of the group and ensure that awareness of ELs is at the forefront in the analysis and interpretation of data.

Stage 8: Data Interpretation

Leadership Team Responsibilities/Actions

Following appropriate professional development, district/school leaders are tasked to facilitate opportunities for accurately and appropriately analyzing and interpreting EL data. Leadership team members must remind teachers and other stakeholders to consider the complex and interactive nature of EL characteristics and data sources.

Teacher Responsibilities/Actions

Based on applying the EL Lens, teachers must work diligently to build an accurate understanding of what ELs know and can do. This requires collaboration, ongoing application of the EL Lens, rethinking the privilege of certain kinds of data, and continuous advocacy for ELs, based on the assumption that they can and will be successful in the classroom if they are provided with the equitable learning opportunities that are mandated in the United States. More essential than simply adhering to legal mandates is enacting the collective will of the district/school to appropriately interpret and apply EL data.

Table 4.2 Contrastive Non-EL and EL. Data Analysis Based on Application of the EL Lens

	Non-EL Lens	EL Lens
Age	The student has had experiences similar to those of age-alike peers and has progressed with those peers through the developmental continuum. Teachers rely on experiences with non-ELs to inform their perceptions of what is "normal" for students at different ages. EXAMPLE: A five-year-old child typically feeds herself.	The experiences and culturally age-appropriate expectations of each child must be examined from a cross-cultural perspective in order to appropriately interpret the data. EXAMPLE: A family requested that a child attend kindergarten near the father's workplace, so he could go to the school to feed her lunch. IMPLICATIONS: Districts/schools must be flexible to meet the cross-cultural needs of families and students.
Grade	A student in ninth grade has progressed through the previous eight grades and kindergarten and performs academically within the range of grade-level peers in terms of content knowledge, skills, and abilities EXAMPLE: A ninth-grade student has already studied US history for many years.	A student may or may not have formal education that is commensurate with that of other ninth graders. He does not perform academically within the range of other ninth graders, though this lack of performance is not indicative of a disability. ***Note that these other ninth graders are not his peers and cannot serve as a basis for comparison.*** EXAMPLE: A student in ninth grade has missed four years of schooling. Further, the education that he did receive was from volunteers in a refugee camp, rather than from certified teachers. No books or other teaching materials were available. (Children wrote in the dirt using sticks in their first language.) The student is not prepared to participate in ninth-grade US history designed for non-ELs. IMPLICATIONS: It is incumbent upon districts/schools to provide instruction that fills in gaps based on student data, and that prepares the student to participate in grade-level classes. Course selection must be based on the student's ability to participate to the extent necessary for him to benefit from the class.

	Non-EL Lens	EL Lens
Family Background	Students come from a range of family backgrounds, including two-parent homes, single-parent homes, and homes with many other configurations. It is generally assumed that students live with an adult who acts as a guardian. EXAMPLE: A high school student lives with her mother during the week and with her father on weekends.	Students may come from a wider range of family backgrounds and may even be unaccompanied. EXAMPLE: A high school student lives alone in an apartment. When ill, he must report his own absence, which goes against the school policy (parents/guardians must report absences). IMPLICATIONS: Policies must be adjusted from time to time in order to encompass the realities of ELs to promote their success in the school environment.
Country of Origin	The preponderance of non-ELs were born in the United States. EXAMPLE: A student was born in Alabama, but, after moving with his family, attends elementary school in Massachusetts.	The US student population reflects a growing number of countries of origin and first languages. However, the majority of K–12 ELs in US schools were born in the United States. EXAMPLE: A student comes to the United States from El Salvador and is awaiting a trial to determine if she can stay, while another EL from El Salvador is a third-generation US citizen. IMPLICATIONS: Understanding students' countries of origin and associated circumstances can provide teachers with critical information essential to meeting their needs.
Immigrant/ Refugee/ Migrant/Other Status	Most non-ELs in US schools possess US citizenship and have access to various supports and entitlements when needed (e.g., Medicaid, food stamps). EXAMPLE: A family's breadwinner loses a job. The family can take advantage of various entitlements until another job is secured.	Many ELs may not be aware of or have access to supports and entitlements. Further, those ELs lacking documentation are not entitled to receive those supports. EXAMPLE: A newcomer family, recently arrived as part of the national refugee family reunification program, has no entitlements, despite coming to the United States through legal channels. IMPLICATIONS: Newcomers may experience challenges related to basic physical needs (e.g., medical care, food). These needs must be met, and educators are well positioned to connect families and students with appropriate resources or to create awareness of such need to mount a collective response.

(Continued)

Table 4.2 (Continued)

	Non-EL Lens	EL Lens
Living Situation (e.g., housing, homelessness)	In many US homes, each child has his or her own bedroom or shares a room with one or two other siblings. EXAMPLE: A family with three children (two girls and one boy) lives in a three-bedroom apartment where the parents have their own bedroom, the girls share a room, and the boy has his own bedroom. All three children have their own desks for study purposes.	Some newcomer families live with another family upon arrival in a new community to conserve resources. These arrangements may be temporary or more long term. EXAMPLE: Two or three single-parent families totaling 17 people join together in a small apartment in subsidized housing. There is a lack of furniture (including beds) and further, no space for children to have their own study spaces. IMPLICATIONS: Challenging living situations may impact students in many ways (e.g., lack of resources, tiredness). Specifically, homework expectations must be aligned with students' home situations as described, as well as their ability to gain homework assistance.
Socioeconomic Status (e.g., food security)	K–12 students in US schools have the right to apply for free or reduced-price lunches and often breakfasts at school. EXAMPLE: A student with low socioeconomic status participates in the free breakfast and lunch programs at her school.	ELs may not know about the process of obtaining free or reduced-price meals and may go without meals if the family cannot provide for them. EXAMPLE: An EL with low socioeconomic status comes to school without breakfast and does not eat lunch, since her parents cannot provide it. IMPLICATIONS: Caring school personnel must ensure that all children eat every day without being stigmatized, regardless of their socioeconomic status. Families may not realize that a Social Security number is *not* required on the application for free or reduced-price meals. Further, food choices that match religious needs (e.g., fish on Friday during Lent or pork-free choices) must be provided as a matter of course, as needed.
Cultural Background/ Practices	Most non-EL children come from families that engage in Western medical practices. EXAMPLE: A child with body aches/flu is given over-the-counter medication.	Many non-US cultures engage in medical practices outside of the Western tradition. EXAMPLE: A child with body aches/flu is treated by a parent using "coining," during which a coin or other similar metal object is dragged over the skin of

	Non-EL Lens	EL Lens
		the affected part of the body (e.g., the back). This results in long bruises that might be mistaken for or reported as a form of child abuse.
		IMPLICATIONS: Cultural sensitivity is required when reporting concerns about child abuse. Careful consideration of folk or homeopathic remedies is essential in supporting families as they learn to live in a new culture. Mandatory reporters must become informed about such practices and their intent.
Educational Backgrounds	Most non-ELs participate consistently in K–12 schools that offer fairly similar curricular learning opportunities. EXAMPLE: A child starts fifth grade with background knowledge in science that is similar to that of his new grade-level peers.	Some ELs experience gaps in their education or even no education at all prior to arriving in the United States. EXAMPLE: An EL starts fifth grade having never attended school before. School-based experiences such as science experiments are entirely new to this student. His background knowledge about science is likely to be quite different from that of his new grade-level peers. IMPLICATIONS: Educational gaps must be addressed with programming designed for ELs, rather than with remedial programming designed for students who have had previous opportunities to learn the given content. This may require that new programs be created for ELs with limited formal schooling.
First Language/ Script	Most non-ELs have grown up with consistent environmental exposure to the Latin script, which is also used at school. EXAMPLE: Kindergarten students can often write their names.	Some ELs have had little to no experience with written language, even in their first language. Others have learned writing systems that make use of non-Latin alphabets or characters, and they are unfamiliar with the Latin script. EXAMPLE: Newcomer ELs of any age may be able to write their names in the script of their first language but not with Latin script, or they may not be able to write their names at all.

(Continued)

Table 4.2 (Continued)

	Non-EL Lens	EL Lens
		IMPLICATIONS: Regardless of the age of the student, each EL must be provided meaningful pre-reading/writing and literacy instruction with the same intensity and regularity that their non-EL counterparts received during their initial phases of learning to read. Remedial programs for non-ELs are not indicated; rather, ELs need literacy instruction that targets their specific, emergent learning-to-read needs.
First Language Listening/ Speaking Levels	Most non-ELs in the United States have grown up speaking English, following a generally predictable language development trajectory. EXAMPLE: An eight-year-old non-EL can produce extended speech that is similar to that of other non-ELs with similar backgrounds who have grown up in the United States	Most ELs have grown up speaking their first language, following a generally predictable language development trajectory. EXAMPLE: An eight-year-old EL can produce extended speech that is similar to that of other ELs with similar backgrounds who have grown up in the same area. Nevertheless, differences in the ways that children are engaged in interactions with and by adults, and norms for those interactions, vary greatly across cultures. IMPLICATIONS: Listening and speaking in English are generally precursors to the development of reading and writing in English. Therefore, listening and speaking skills in English must be explicitly taught.
First Language Reading/ Writing Levels	Most non-ELs in the United States make approximately one year's growth in English reading and writing during each year that they attend school. EXAMPLE: With English reading and writing instruction typically geared to the needs of non-ELs, a fourth grader is expected to make one year's growth in reading and writing during fourth grade.	ELs who enter school must make larger gains than their non-EL peers in order to attain grade-level performance in English. For this reason, their peer group is *not* the non-ELs in their given grade; rather, the peer group must be recognized to be other ELs with similar linguistic, cultural, and experiential backgrounds. EXAMPLE: A fourth grade EL speaker of Kikuyu from Kenya is reading at the third grade level in English, having been in the United States for one year. Rather than needing special education programming, as his teachers suggest, this child is likely gifted and may benefit from specific programming that develops his talents.

	Non-EL Lens	EL Lens
		IMPLICATIONS: The language development trajectory for ELs is different from the trajectory of non-ELs; this reality is not indicative of cognitive impairment. Rather, achievement of grade-level expectations requires that ELs learn faster than their non-EL peers. The accomplishment of grade-level expectations must be recognized as an extraordinary accomplishment, particularly considering the first language skills that ELs have already developed.
Length of Time in the U.S.	Most non-ELs have spent most of their lives in the United States. EXAMPLE: A seventh-grade non-EL has grown up on a farm in the Midwest that has been in his family for generations.	Most ELs have spent their entire lives in the United States, although many have come from all over the world and have been in the United States for varying lengths of time. EXAMPLE: A seventh-grade EL whose parents arrived as refugees before his birth represents a second generation of English learner, but he is not fully proficient in English. Another seventh-grade EL from Burma has recently arrived from a refugee camp in Thailand and already has some English language skills due to learning in the refugee camp. IMPLICATIONS: The length of time that an EL has been in the United States is not always directly indicative of the student's instructional needs nor what the student brings to the classroom. Some ELs spend multiple years in the United States, but their English language proficiency stagnates at a low level due to a lack of targeted instruction. Others who have been in the United States for shorter periods of time achieve advanced English language development. Length of time in the United States must be considered within the context of the bigger picture of each student's individual background characteristics, rather than as a factor that automatically results in advanced or proficient levels of English language development.

(Continued)

Table 4.2 (Continued)

	Non-EL Lens	EL Lens
English Listening/ Speaking Levels	Having been exposed to English since birth, most non-ELs are capable of interacting using spoken English. EXAMPLE: A native-English-speaking kindergartener can easily negotiate the daily routines of school (e.g., getting lunch, making simple requests).	Having had varying exposure to English, ELs are generally less capable of interacting in English than non-ELs. EXAMPLE: A newcomer to the United States is unlikely to be proficient in spoken English and may even be silent. IMPLICATIONS: Educators need to recognize the predictable, incremental process of developing listening and speaking skills in English. This comprehensive task requires that all teachers view themselves as language teachers for the ELs in their classrooms.
English Reading/ Writing Levels	Most non-ELs in the United States make approximately one year's growth in English reading and writing during each year that they attend school, one and the same as their first-language development. EXAMPLE: With English reading and writing instruction typically geared to the needs of non-ELs, a seventh grader is expected to make one year's growth in reading and writing during seventh grade.	Having a lack of proficiency in spoken English, along with a possible lack of literacy skills in the first language, ELs can appear to be less capable of reading and writing in English than non-ELs in the same grade level. EXAMPLE: A newcomer seventh-grade EL, who tested at Level 1 in all English language domains, attended school in Somalia for a total of two years. The student speaks Somali but is unable to read or write it well. This student cannot derive meaning from grade-level content reading in English. IMPLICATIONS: Students benefit from targeted English language instruction focused on reading and writing, supported by leveled materials aligned with grade-level content. These students should not automatically be placed in special education nor subjected to computer-based interventions not designed for ELs. Further, students who have limited or no instruction in reading their first language cannot be expected to glean meaning from materials written in this language.
Exposure to English Outside of School	Most non-ELs benefit from constant exposure to English in the neighborhood, in the media, et cetera. EXAMPLE: A high school non-EL hears English all around him, both during and after school.	Many ELs are not exposed to English in their home environments. EXAMPLE: A high school EL from Honduras lives in an enclave community where his family conducts business at Spanish-speaking stores,

	Non-EL Lens	EL Lens
	Environmental print in the home includes magazines, newspapers, grocery lists, et cetera. All conversations, music, TV, and Internet-based communication take place in English. He can seek out assistance with homework from family members who speak, read, and write English.	watches Spanish-language TV, and speaks Spanish at home. IMPLICATIONS: Some ELs do not have opportunities to practice and develop language skills outside of school. Further, their families cannot help them with homework. Ongoing production of both social and academic English must take place within the school day with embedded opportunities for interaction.
Standardized Test Data in the Content Areas	Realizing that a standardized test score is but a snapshot in time, these scores are meant to be indicators of what students know and can do in the content areas. While a student may simply not be a good test taker or have a bad day, in general, the reliability indices and validity arguments for such tests support their use as data points for non-ELs. EXAMPLE: A second grader scores in the 76th percentile on a national measure of social studies. This means that she scored well above average on that particular measure.	ELs' scores on standardized achievement tests are difficult to interpret, since the content to be tested is confounded with the English language. This means that it is impossible to ascertain whether a score indicates an EL's content understanding, her language ability in English, or both. For this reason, these scores tend not to accurately estimate what ELs know and can do in the content areas and often underestimate ELs' knowledge, skills, and abilities. Even a mathematical computation test may be challenging to ELs who know math well, due to differences in mathematical symbols and problem-solving approaches in various countries. EXAMPLE: A second-grade EL scores at the 8th percentile on the same national measure of social studies. This means that the student scored well below average. However, it is impossible to tell if this score is due to a lack of social studies knowledge, a lack of ability to read English, or both. It is to be expected that ELs would not necessarily perform especially well on tests conducted in English. IMPLICATIONS: Large-scale standardized achievement testing is not generally designed with ELs in mind. Rather, tests are retrofitted (e.g., through the use of accommodations) when used with ELs. For this reason, these scores cannot and should not be

(Continued)

Table 4.2 (Continued)

	Non-EL Lens	EL Lens
		trusted as accurate indicators of what ELs know and can do in the content areas. An accurate understanding of the academic achievement of ELs can be gained only through other means (e.g., creative, teacher-developed classroom assessments).
Grades/Grade Point Average	Teachers have traditionally had considerable autonomy in determining the factors that influence grades (e.g., content achievement, effort, behavior, attendance). The increasing emphasis on standards-based grading has clarified the meaning of grades, as nonacademic factors such as behavior and attendance are not to be included in content area grades. EXAMPLE: A ninth grader's report card indicates a grade of B for language arts. The card further lists individual grades for writing (C), grammar (B), reading (B), and oral communication (A-). Standards are provided for each area of language arts, and clarification of the meaning of the letter grades (e.g., A = standard met, B = standard nearly met) is also provided.	As a whole, there seems to be considerable confusion about the grading of ELs. Some teachers, feeling sorry for the continual challenges that their students face, grant an "A for effort." Others, who have been told that ELs must be taught to the same standards as non-ELs, find themselves awarding mostly Ds and Fs to these students. EXAMPLE: An EL ninth grader's report card shows mostly Ds and Fs. The parents are concerned that their child is not learning at all. However, conferences with teachers reveal that the student works hard in class and is making significant progress, but that she hasn't met grade-level benchmarks. IMPLICATIONS: Since the purpose of grading is to share information with students and parents about learning, efforts must be made to ensure that grades provide an accurate accounting of student learning. See Chapter 5 for further discussion.
Benchmarks (i.e., incremental levels of achievement within a grade level that are to be met on the way to mastery of a standard)	Benchmarks are designed for non-ELs, as part of expected progressions within a grade level in specific content areas. EXAMPLE: A sixth-grade non-EL meets the fall benchmark in reading, falls short of the winter benchmark, receives a short intervention, and meets the spring benchmark.	Given that benchmarks are designed for non-ELs, they may likely be developmentally inappropriate for ELs. That is, these benchmarks do not take into account the trajectory of EL learning, nor where ELs currently perform on the continuum of English language and content development. EXAMPLE: A sixth-grade EL falls short of meeting all of the benchmarks in reading throughout the year. IMPLICATION: Flexibility is essential in the determination of appropriate benchmarks for ELs and the design of

	Non-EL Lens	EL Lens
		scaffolded instruction. Educators must bear in mind that grade level, English language development level, and content achievement are three separate aspects of school-based learning that are uniquely intertwined, yet distinct, for ELs.
Behaviors (e.g., inattentiveness, aggression, inappropriate behavior, withdrawn demeanor, lack of eye contact)	Behaviors of non-ELs might indicate needs that are familiar and often interpreted in culturally bound ways. EXAMPLES: inattentiveness = attention deficit disorder (ADD) inappropriate behavior (e.g., urinating on school grounds during recess) = a sign of disrespect aggression = oppositional defiant disorder withdrawn demeanor = depression lack of eye contact = disregard/ disrespect or lying	Behaviors of ELs might have different interpretations, given different reasons for those behaviors. EXAMPLES: inattentiveness = lack of understanding in English inappropriate behavior (e.g., urinating on school grounds during recess) = lack of background knowledge related to school expectations (the refugee student did not have access to adequate restroom facilities in the refugee camp) aggression = learned survival behavior (the refugee student had to defend his food and limited property in the camp in order to maintain possession of it) withdrawn demeanor = post-traumatic stress disorder (the student witnessed or experienced traumatic events during her migration to the United States from Central America) lack of eye contact = respect for elders or those in authority IMPLICATIONS: Teachers must be inquisitive about all EL behaviors, searching for explanations that take into account linguistic, cultural, and experiential differences.
Pronunciation/ Accent (e.g., inaccurate sounds, inappropriate sounds)	Non-ELs who exhibit nonstandard pronunciation are often referred for speech services. EXAMPLE: A fifth-grade non-EL who speaks with a lisp receives services from a speech language pathologist.	ELs often pronounce words in different ways than non-ELs as they are learning a new language. Further, some facets of pronunciation never achieve "native speaker" status; however, this is not generally indicative of a speech disorder that requires intervention. The sounds of a student's first language will influence her pronunciation in English; she will easily pronounce some sounds but may mispronounce new, unfamiliar sounds in English, resulting in

Table 4.2 (Continued)

	Non-EL Lens	EL Lens
		predictable interference errors (e.g., some ELs cannot pronounce the *th* sound [as in *thin*], substituting the *t* or *s* sound instead). Such errors should not be counted against her as she develops her English speaking and oral reading skills.
		EXAMPLE: A perplexed teacher describes her Iraqi fifth-grade student, who has been in the United States for less than a year, as producing "inappropriate sounds" and then running from the classroom. Further investigation reveals that the Farsi-speaking EL was frustrated when trying to pronounce a series of decontextualized vowel digraphs as part of her phonics development intervention in English. Because the letter-sound correspondence had never been taught, and since many of the sounds do not exist in her native Farsi, the decontextualized activity was neither meaningful nor productive for the EL and in fact only overwhelmed her.
		IMPLICATIONS: Instruction must be contextualized and meaningful for ELs. Further, teachers should familiarize themselves with the basic components of their students' first languages in order to understand predictable errors[1]. Finally, students should never be tested on skills and knowledge that have not been taught.
Classroom Performance	Expert teachers who differentiate for students often have a better sense of non-ELs' knowledge, skills, and abilities in their content areas than a single standardized test score can communicate.	Expert teachers who differentiate for students often have a better sense of ELs' knowledge, skills, and abilities in their content areas than a single standardized test score can communicate.
	EXAMPLE: Because a teacher has observed a non-EL's demonstrations in the classroom, she is confident the student fully understands, can sequence, and can describe a chemical reaction.	EXAMPLE: Because a teacher has observed an EL's demonstrations in the classroom, she is confident the student fully understands, can sequence, and can describe a chemical reaction.

[1]Interested teachers can gain insight into the features of numerous languages and the ways in which they differ from English by consulting the resources at the end of the chapter.

	Non-EL Lens	EL Lens
		IMPLICATIONS: Classroom performance should be weighted more heavily and afforded the significance that it merits, rather than relying on other less accurate sources of information (e.g., standardized achievement test scores) when analyzing student data.
Information From Parents, Cultural Informants, and Home Visits	Parents of non-ELs are routinely encouraged to become involved in school activities, to support their children's learning at home, to attend various school functions, et cetera. This positions non-EL parents to actively contribute to teachers' work with their children. In addition, non-EL parents are likely to seek clarification, question, and advocate for their children. EXAMPLE: Homeroom parents respond to a note sent home from school asking that they support the classroom through ongoing volunteer efforts, such as cutting laminated materials.	EL parents are an often-overlooked resource in terms of understanding entry points for the instruction of ELs. They need to be encouraged and empowered to become involved in their children's schooling experiences in the same ways that non-EL parents are. In addition, gaps in background information about ELs can be filled during parent interviews, which can clarify parental insights and expectations regarding their children. In addition, cultural informants (e.g., bilingual paraeducators/associates, community members) can provide perspectives on cultural factors that impact student behavior and performance, acting as a support to the data analysis process. In addition, home visits by educators can inform perceptions through first-hand observations, making data analysis more accurate and valuable. EXAMPLE: In response to culturally appropriate invitations and supports (e.g., phone call in the language they best understand, transportation, child care), a morning group for volunteer EL parents provides ways for EL parents to support the classroom teacher, such as cutting laminated materials or reading aloud a bilingual book to students.
Student Interests	Non-ELs have interests that can be capitalized upon to enhance motivation and engagement. EXAMPLE: A 10th-grade student is acting out in the classroom. The teacher, knowing his interest and talent in art, asks that he support	ELs have interests that can be capitalized upon to enhance motivation and engagement. EXAMPLE: ELs who are nervous about presenting speeches to peers in English can draw upon their own cultural areas of expertise to boost their confidence.

(Continued)

Table 4.2 (Continued)

	Non-EL Lens	EL Lens
	her and the rest of the students by creating sketches that represent important content concepts. The student rises to the occasion, is appreciated by both teacher and classmates, and becomes engaged in learning.	For example, a Bosnian student presents a speech focusing on a process about how to grind, brew, and serve traditional Bosnian coffee, using the tools his family brought with them from Klujc. IMPLICATIONS: In the same way that teachers capitalize upon the interests of non-ELs, they can draw upon ELs' interests and cultural insights as a springboard for language development, engagement in learning, and the reciprocal development of cultural competence shared by ELs and non-ELs.
Other Factors (e.g., giftedness, learning disabilities, physical disabilities)	Non-ELs are identified for specialized programming using assessments that were designed for them and within a cultural context that is likely to be familiar to them. EXAMPLE: A non-EL is identified for gifted/talented programming based on parental advocacy in addition to a range of assessment data.	ELs are often misidentified for specialized programming or are not identified at all, given that assessments are designed for non-ELs and are not sensitive to the unique characteristics of ELs. Generally, ELs should be identified at a rate that is neither higher nor lower than that of non-ELs in specialized programming. EXAMPLE: An EL is misidentified as in need of special education based only on her developing, but below grade level, ability to read in English. In contrast, no ELs are identified for participating in gifted/talented programming. IMPLICATIONS: Schools and districts must recognize alternate ways to identify ELs for gifted programming, given that standardized test scores often underestimate what ELs know and can do. That is, the EL Lens must be applied to the analysis of all data in order to ensure appropriate and equitable placement of ELs in programming that is designed to meet their needs.

Other Stakeholder Responsibilities/Actions

Other stakeholders must adopt the EL Lens approach to data interpretation, which allows previously undervalued sources of information about students to gain their rightful status in illuminating what ELs know and can do. As part of the unified and collective will of the district/school to provide ELs with parity of access to standards-based achievement, other stakeholders must champion the application of the EL Lens across district/school endeavors.

Stage 9: Data-Driven Action

Grounded in accurate analysis of student data, administrators, teachers, and other stakeholders can move forward in the process of engaging students in standards-based content instruction in accordance with their current English language development levels.

Leadership Team Responsibilities/Actions

District/school leaders must ensure that teachers have the materials needed to engage ELs in standards-based learning, taking into account their individual English language development levels. This will likely require the provision of supplementary differentiated materials that align with content standards.

Teacher Responsibilities/Actions

Based on accurate interpretations of EL data, teachers are poised to target standards-based instruction to students' individual English language development levels, using a variety of print, digital, technological, and other materials appropriate to students' individual language levels. This process will be outlined in detail in the following chapter.

Other Stakeholder Responsibilities/Actions

Other stakeholders must embrace the collective responsibility to provide ELs with access to standards-based learning. This may include advocacy or support for the purchase of materials that simultaneously reinforce language and content learning and that result in affording ELs parity of access.

Stage 10: Ongoing Support

Leadership Team Responsibilities/Actions

As teachers work to implement data-driven practice, district/school leaders are charged with supporting these endeavors. Supporting teachers in this way may mean

- providing common planning time for teams of teachers;
- recognizing that scope and sequence documents that are provided by publishers of teaching materials may need to be altered in order to ensure student learning;

- supporting teachers willing to reciprocally mentor each other, coteach, and collaborate in creative ways;
- being flexible in allowing teachers to use professional development time to apply learning from professional development sessions they've already attended (rather than using this time for additional professional development sessions);
- developing accountability measures in ways that honor the implementation of the EL Lens;
- holding teachers accountable ways that recognize and expect the application of the EL Lens; and/or
- using data in supportive rather than punitive ways (e.g., providing teachers with additional resources in areas where they need assistance, such as the incorporation of visual supports during instruction).

Expert leaders are limited only by their imaginations in providing needed supports to their creative teachers for designing meaningful and comprehensible ways to engage ELs in their various classroom contexts.

In addition, nonteaching staff must be afforded necessary resources in order to facilitate their engagement. Such resources might include translations of relevant documents and instruction in key words/phrases in various languages (e.g., "This is where you get off the bus" for transportation staff).

Teacher Responsibilities/Actions

Teachers need to build capacity among themselves through collaborating, working in professional learning communities, sharing expertise, and sharing tasks associated with the application of the EL Lens to data analysis and subsequent instruction.

Other Stakeholder Responsibilities/Actions

Other stakeholders must keep their fingers on the pulse of ELs in the district/school with a constantly evolving awareness of newly arriving populations and related community impact. In this way, other stakeholders can support administrators' and teachers' ongoing efforts to welcome, include, and serve ELs and their families district-/school-wide to the extent that they do so for non-ELs.

Stage 11: Feedback

Leadership Team Responsibilities/Actions

District/school leaders must provide timely and relevant feedback to teachers about their application of the EL Lens based on their own growing understanding. This can be accomplished in a variety of ways, including

- bringing in experts to assist teachers with applying the EL Lens,
- supporting the implementation of professional learning communities and/or book studies that target specific topics requested by teachers,
- encouraging teachers to observe and provide feedback to each other in the application of the EL Lens to data analysis,
- recognizing that implementing change is an ongoing process that requires a team spirit, meeting with teachers about concerns and successes, and/or
- grounding high expectations of teachers in the collective will and shared district/school vision, while holding teachers accountable for applying the EL Lens to data analysis.

Leadership team members can provide teachers with feedback in a variety of creative ways to help promote a positive and collegial atmosphere that encourages innovation, acknowledges mistakes as important aspects of improvement, and values all efforts. Feedback must also be provided to other district/school staff involved in the education of ELs.

Teacher Responsibilities/Actions

Teachers must be open to giving and receiving feedback and coaching designed to improve their practice. In fact, teachers are often well positioned to offer insightful feedback to one another, particularly when the feedback is supported with shared coaching strategies or approaches universally relied upon.

Other Stakeholder Responsibilities/Actions

Acknowledging that feedback is an essential aspect of the cycle of continuous improvement, other stakeholders will encourage and support administrators and teachers in carrying out this critical step.

Stage 12: Sharing/Publication of Progress

Leadership Team Responsibilities/Actions

District/school leaders must keep educators and stakeholders informed on the overall application of the EL Lens. Their leadership perspective affords administrators a "balcony" view that allows them to contextualize district/school innovations, successes, and points for potential improvement. This input assists in applying the EL Lens routinely in district-/school-based practice.

Teacher Responsibilities/Actions

Teachers must be willing to share points of pride and accomplishments with one another and with other stakeholders and the larger community. For example, along with students, they might share results of their efforts with the school board.

Other Stakeholder Responsibilities/Actions

Other stakeholders should cultivate an awareness of the EL Lens within the wider community and consistently seek out ways to incorporate and include the EL perspective beyond the district/school doors.

Step 13: Next Steps

Leadership Team Responsibilities/Actions

Leadership team members are charged with determining next steps in the process of continually improving the implementation of the EL Lens at the district/school level. This requires an unrelenting, sustained effort toward the accurate interpretation and use of data for providing access to standards-based instruction.

Teacher Responsibilities/Actions

As a result of *Lau v. Nichols* (1974), teachers are charged to provide ELs parity of access to standards-based achievement as their basic civil right. This mandate can be accomplished only through accurately interpreting EL data and responding accordingly. By basing instructional decisions on appropriate EL data, teachers will be able to linguistically differentiate instruction and assessment of these students, resulting in meeting the requirement to afford ELs access. These processes will be described in detail in Chapters 5 and 6.

Other Stakeholder Responsibilities/Actions

Other stakeholders are called upon to expect and support the application of the EL Lens to data analysis and interpretation. They are called to ask the hard questions that hold others accountable for accurate team-based interpretation and application of EL data.

An opportunity to practice data analysis using the EL Lens is offered in Exercise 4.1 at the end of the chapter. Possible interpretations are suggested following the description of Mee Thaw, a student from Myanmar, formerly Burma. A blank template for use by districts/schools in analyzing individual EL data can be found in Resource 4.1 at the end of the chapter.

EXERCISE 4.1 Practice Data Analysis Using the EL Lens

The following exercise can be used by districts/schools as they learn to apply the EL Lens to data analysis. Suggested interpretations for the data are presented following the exercise.

Directions: Analyze the student data for Mee Thaw, writing your interpretations in the far right column.

Applying the EL Lens: Interpretation of Student Data

Student Name: ___Mee Thaw_____

	Guiding Questions	Student Data	Interpretation
Age	Is the student the same age as others in the class? Why or why not? Can placement be appropriately made with approximately same-age peers? Is the student progressing at the same rate as others who are age-level peers in language development?	18 years old	
Grade	Does the student have academic background built in the first language (L1) that is on grade level?	Ninth grade	
Family Background	Is the student living with her or his intact family? If not, what is the situation? What implications might it have for school success?	Living with three sisters and mother	
Country of Origin, Country of Domicile	Is the country of origin one that suggests the student may have experienced trauma, loss, family separation, migration, or other difficult experiences? Has the student lived outside of the country of origin? If so, what are the impacts?	Burmese national origin, living in Thailand. Mee Thaw was born in a refugee camp in Thailand after her parents fled a violent campaign in Burma (Myanmar). She has never lived in the country of her national origin.	
Immigrant/ Refugee/Migrant/ Other Status	Has the student or family fled for their lives? Might the family benefit from additional support related to this experience?	Refugee	

(Continued)

EXERCISE 4.1 (Continued)

	Guiding Questions	Student Data	Interpretation
Living Situation (e.g., housing, homelessness)	Does the student have safe housing with a support system of adults?	Yes	
Socioeconomic Status (e.g., food security)	When the school week is over and school lunch programs do not operate, does the student have sufficient food? Does the student have material and medical needs met?	Yes	
Cultural Background/ Practices	Has the staff been informed of cultural or health practices of this student that they might wonder about?	Yes	
Educational Backgrounds	Are the parents of the student literate in their L1? Can the student read in the L1? Is the student on grade level in the L1? Has the student attended school previously? Where? In what grades? Does the student have a transcript that can be translated to afford credit for classes taken?	Mee Thaw's mother is literate in Karen at the elementary level. The student can read minimally in her L1 and has no transcript from a previous school.	
First Language/ Script	Does the student's L1 utilize the Latin script, or is another writing system used? What implications does this information have for literacy instruction in English? What implications might exist for handwriting instruction?	The Karen language does not rely on the Latin script. Implications for instruction include the need for prereading activities in rhyming, songs, chanting, segmentation, et cetera, followed by contextualized vocabulary and targeted reading development in English, even though the student is 18 years old. This type of reading instruction, which is frequently called for, must be informed by the EL Lens.	

	Guiding Questions	**Student Data**	**Interpretation**
First Language Listening/ Speaking Levels	Can the student interact with others in the L1? Is the EL on par with other ELs of the same age and experience?	The EL exhibits listening/speaking skills commensurate with those of age-level peers from the same refugee camp in Thailand.	
First Language Reading/Writing Levels	Can the student write his or her name in the L1? A sentence? A paragraph? Can the student read in the L1?	The EL can write her name in Karen, but cannot yet generate a sentence independently. The student is able to read Karen text at the word/ phrase level.	
Length of Time in the United States	How long has the student lived in the United States? Where did the student live before that? What were the living conditions? What has the student experienced in the United States?	Mee Thaw has lived in the United States for six months. In the Thai refugee camp, she lived in a modest hut with a dirt floor and without running water, electrical appliances, or other modern conveniences. In the United States, she first lived in a large city in the East and subsequently moved with her family to the Midwest. Her experiences in the United States have been extremely limited.	
English Listening/ Speaking Levels	Can the student understand simple questions in English? Can the student point to objects or follow simple directions in English? What information does the English language development assessment provide about levels of language?	The student is highly motivated and enthusiastically participates in interaction that involves listening and speaking in English. She is very quickly acquiring contextualized words and phrases that match her needs for expression.	

(Continued)

EXERCISE 4.1 (Continued)

	Guiding Questions	Student Data	Interpretation
English Reading/ Writing Levels	Can the student read in the L1? Can the student read in English? What is the student's guided reading level in English? What is the student's grade level in US schools? Is there a difference between the L1 reading level and the English reading level? What actions might a difference between the EL's grade level and reading/ writing level call for?	This relative newcomer is ready to learn to read in English and will require explicit, targeted reading development that recognizes her maturity, yet engages her in the earliest phases of learning to read and write in English.	
Exposure to English Outside of School	To what extent does the student interact in English at home? To what extent does the student interact in English before and after school? Does the student have a job that requires using English? Does the student have English-speaking friends outside of school? Does the student live in an enclave community where English is not needed?	Mee Thaw has secured a job at the mall, which will greatly support her oral English language learning, which will in turn support her learning to read and write in English. In addition, she has a circle of friends from the International Club at school that socializes outside of school.	
Standardized Test Data in the Content Areas	Has the student received content instruction in English? What are the English language development levels of the student? Can those levels predict what the student can understand in terms of the standardized assessment questions? What else is evident from these data about this EL, and what cannot be determined? What are the implications for language instruction for this student?	As a newcomer, Mee Thaw receives an exemption for 12 months from taking a standardized Reading assessment, but is required to take the math section. Knowing that she performs at Level 2 in Reading in English, Mee Thaw is unable to derive meaning from grade-level print. As a result, teachers can predict the likelihood of a low score on these assessments due to the English language barrier.	

	Guiding Questions	Student Data	Interpretation
Grades/Grade Point Average	Is there a district policy in place for grading ELs? Does the grading policy embody an additive view of ELs? Is the grading policy differentiated based on differentiated language development levels of the EL? Do the grades provide accurate and meaningful information to this student and family? Are the grades based on (modified) content standards? Are report card comments meaningful to this student and family?	Mee Thaw is enrolled in high school, where her teachers are differentiating her content assignments and materials based on her English language development levels. She is performing well within the levels indicated by her data. Her teachers are modifying ninth-grade standards for her, implementing differentiated instruction designed to scaffold her learning, and implementing differentiated grading. Mee is earning an A in her social studies class, with a report card notation of "differentiated grading."	
Benchmarks (i.e., incremental levels of achievement within a grade level that are to be met on the way to mastery of a standard)	Does the district/school embrace the notion that ELs who are placed in a specific grade might not be able to perform at grade level due to a variety of factors? Does the district/school recognize that background must be built for ELs who have experienced a lack of opportunity to learn? Does the district/school embrace the fact that a lack of opportunity to learn does not constitute a cognitive deficit or a need for special education, but rather a need for targeted instruction that meets the EL at an appropriate instructional level?	At the age of 18, Mee Thaw is older than her grade-level peers, but thanks to her forward-thinking school district administrators, teachers, and stakeholders, Mee Thaw has an opportunity to maximize her high school experience, earn credits, and even to graduate by the end of her 21st year. Her learning has been measured in relation to her own growth, rather than against a superimposed model based on grade-level progressions in which Mee Thaw has not been able to participate.	

(Continued)

EXERCISE 4.1 (Continued)

	Guiding Questions	Student Data	Interpretation
Behaviors (e.g., inattentiveness, aggression, inappropriate behavior, withdrawn demeanor, lack of eye contact)	Do all stakeholders operate from an open-minded position that first asks and investigates, rather than judges and stereotypes, when the behaviors of this student are different from those of non-ELs? Have stakeholders received professional development that helps them to interpret any misunderstood behaviors of this student through an EL Lens? Have all stakeholders adopted an orientation of advocacy for this student?	When Mee Thaw appeared at school with an opaque mixture of ground tree bark and water on both sides of her face, curiosity of both staff and students was piqued. Research and inquiry revealed that this cultural cosmetic is applied to enhance beauty. Eventually, Mee Thaw's circle of non-EL friends tried the practice, known as "thanakha."	
Pronunciation/ Accent (e.g., inaccurate sounds, "inappropriate" sounds)	When discussing characteristics of this student, are stakeholders able to identify ethnocentric attitudes and vocabulary that communicate negative perceptions? Are district/school stakeholders committed to setting high expectations for this student?	Mee Thaw's pronunciation in English is predictable, based on a contrastive analysis of sounds in Karen. Her school has incorporated the languages of students into a global studies class that positions ELs as experts to teach useful words and phrases to their classmates, EL and non-EL alike.	
Classroom Performance	Has the EL lived in a culture that encourages competition and outspoken views? Has the EL lived in a culture that promotes success of the group over the success of an individual? Is the EL comfortable asking questions of teachers? Might this EL tend to support others in school work or tests as a means of supporting the group?	Mee Thaw has been socialized in a collectivistic culture, which means that her actions must be understood in the context of her whole group. She is unlikely to distinguish herself as an individual by offering answers; she believes it is disrespectful to ask questions of her teacher. Mee Thaw's efforts to assist her peers could possibly be misconstrued as cheating.	

	Guiding Questions	**Student Data**	**Interpretation**
Information From Parents, Cultural Informants, and Home Visits	Is there a formal structure in place that provides routine communication with this student's parents, both in written forms and also by telephone? Is there a communication center that these parents can call to report absences, check on their student, et cetera, using their first languages? Are these parents consistently involved in school activities through school-based efforts to be welcoming and inclusive? Are there expectations that teachers will conduct home visits and form relationships with these parents? Are teachers rewarded for those efforts? Are there enough bilingual associates, tutors, teachers, or outreach workers to meet the needs of this family to the same extent that the needs of non-EL families are met?	Since there is a shortage of Karen interpreters, the school district has hired Mee Thaw's older sister part time to contact Karen-speaking families with school news, to invite them to school events, to report absences, and to schedule home visits.	
Student Interests	Do teachers infuse this student's interests into instruction to motivate and encourage the student to participate in content learning? If appropriate, is this student positioned to assume the role of expert informant? For example, could this student provide reports that focus on her or his country of origin in social studies class?	Mee Thaw's Karen-speaking expertise has been recognized, as she is the "expert" teaching her peers useful words and phrases in her global studies class.	
Other Factors (e.g., giftedness, learning disabilities, physical disabilities)	Has the district/school used means other than standardized assessments to determine whether this student is a candidate for gifted/talented programming? for special education programming?	Soon after her enrollment at high school, Mee Thaw's love of music became apparent. Understanding the value of capitalizing on	

EXERCISE 4.1 (Continued)

	Guiding Questions	Student Data	Interpretation
	Is there clarity about how this student can be served in such programming?	this interest, her counselor enrolled her in the school chorus and also invited her to try instruments in the band room. Mee Thaw picked up a flute and has continued to play it in the band, thanks to an instrument donation program that aims to provide musical instruments to each student who would like to learn to play one.	

SUGGESTED INTERPRETATIONS

Applying the EL Lens: Interpretation of Student Data

Student Name: <u>Mee Thaw</u>

	Guiding Questions	Student Data	Interpretation
Age	Is the student the same age as others in the class? Why or why not? Can placement be appropriately made with approximately same-age peers? Is the student progressing at the same rate as others who are age-level peers in language development?	18 years old	Is the designation of older students as ninth graders imperative? Could a more advanced designation be provided, potentially, for a longer period of time? Mee Thaw is designated a junior for three years. Her advanced age must signal the need for attention to her reading development in English: A comprehensive plan must be implemented to advance her reading level in English, which is well below ninth-grade level.
Grade	Does the student have academic background built in the L1 (first language) that is on grade level?	Ninth grade	Grade level designation is less important than ascertaining the EL's instructional level and providing appropriate instruction that builds missing background and needed literacy skills in English. The English language development levels of students are often not at grade level in English.
Family Background	Is the student living with her or his intact family? If not, what is the situation? What implications might it have for school success?	Living with three sisters and mother	Flexibility in working with family configurations is essential, as is understanding their specific challenges.
Country of Origin, Country of Domicile	Is the country of origin one that suggests the student has experienced trauma, loss, family separation, migration, or other difficult experiences? Has the student lived outside of the country of origin? If so, what are the impacts?	Burmese national origin, living in Thailand. Mee Thaw was born in a refugee camp in Thailand after her parents fled a violent campaign in Burma (Myanmar). She has never lived in the country of her national origin.	Country of origin is often not the same as country of previous residence. This information can explain complicated cultural and linguistic funds of knowledge that students bring with them.

(Continued)

	Guiding Questions	Student Data	Interpretation
Immigrant/ Refugee/ Migrant/Other Status	Has the student or his family fled for their lives? Might the family benefit from additional support related to this experience?	Refugee	Many immigrants and refugees alike have experienced trauma and suffer the attendant negative impact on learning. Sensitive educators and administrators can assist in transitions and can seek out further guidance.
Living Situation (e.g., housing, homelessness)	Does the student have safe housing with a support system of adults?	Yes	Students without the safe environment and support system of adults are severely underresourced and at risk. They are likely to benefit from the focused attention of school staff and stakeholders to ensure that their basic needs are met, paving the way for academic achievement.
Socioeconomic Status (e.g., food security)	When the school week is over and school lunch programs do not operate, does the student have sufficient food? Does the student have material and medical needs met?	Yes	Students without nutritional and medical support will depend on observant and responsive districts/ schools to ensure their well-being.
Cultural Background/ Practices	Has the staff been informed of cultural or health practices of this student that they might wonder about?	Yes	While cultural practices vary widely and may appear eccentric, supportive districts/schools understand that all people have the right to practice their first cultures while learning a new culture.
Educational Backgrounds	Are the parents of the student literate in their L1? Can the student read in the L1? Is the student in grade level in the L1? Has the student attended school previously? Where? In what grades? Does the student have a transcript that can be translated to afford credit for classes taken?	Mee Thaw's mother is literate in Karen at the elementary level. The student can read minimally in her L1 and has no transcript from a previous school.	EL parents of modest educational backgrounds often hold high educational aspirations for their children. If parents are preliterate in their L1, they must receive communication on the L1 (to the extent practicable) via other means (e.g., a phone call from a bilingual associate). Credit should be granted to students who produce transcripts that can be applied toward graduation credits.

	Guiding Questions	Student Data	Interpretation
First Language/ Script	Does the student's L1 utilize the Latin script, or is another writing system used? What implications does this information have for literacy instruction in English? What implications might exist for handwriting instruction?	The Karen language does not rely on the Latin script. Implications for instruction include the need for prereading activities in rhyming, songs, chanting, segmentation, et cetera, followed by contextualized vocabulary and targeted reading development in English, even though the student is 18 years old. This type of reading instruction, which is frequently called for, must be informed by the EL Lens.	The need for appropriate reading/writing instruction is not related to age, but rather to the intersection of the student's English development level and her literacy development in her L1. In this case, grade-level (Grade 9) benchmarks are not reasonable.
First Language Listening/ Speaking Levels	Can the student interact with others in the L1? Is the EL on par with other ELs of the same age and experience?	The EL exhibits listening/ speaking skills commensurate with those of age-level peers from the same refugee camp in Thailand.	Parents are the best resource when seeking information about language abilities in the L1, particularly if there is a sibling for comparison. Such information can be gathered at a home visit, parent conferences, or other meeting supported by a bilingual liaison. When difficulties are reported as taking place in both languages, this is significant information.
First Language Reading/Writing Levels	Can the student write his or her name in the L1? A sentence? A paragraph? Can the student read in the L1?	The EL can write her name in Karen, but cannot yet generate a sentence independently. The student is able to read Karen text at the word/phrase level.	See above.

(Continued)

(Continued)

	Guiding Questions	Student Data	Interpretation
Length of Time in the United States	How long has the student lived in the United States? Where did the student live before that? What were the living conditions? What has the student experienced in the United States?	Mee Thaw has lived in the United States for six months. In the Thai refugee camp, she lived in a modest hut with a dirt floor and without running water, electrical appliances, or other modern conveniences. In the United States, she first lived in a large city in the East and subsequently moved with her family to the Midwest. Her experiences in the United States have been extremely limited.	The length of time in the United States is not necessarily an accurate measure of advanced English language development. Further, assumptions about Mee Thaw's background schema must not be made. Educators can expect a significant need for filling in educational gaps to support Mee Thaw in developing familiarity with her surroundings and American culture. She should also be recognized as an asset to the school for her cultural insight and expertise. Educators should look for ways to engage Mee Thaw in sharing her language, culture, and experiences.
English Listening/ Speaking Levels	Can the student understand simple questions in English? Can the student point to objects or follow simple directions in English? What information does the English language development assessment provide about levels of language?	The student is highly motivated and enthusiastically participates in interaction that involves listening and speaking in English. She is very quickly acquiring contextualized words and phrases that match her needs for expression.	Teachers must capitalize instructionally on the student's interest and rapidly developing ability in English. Provide opportunities for interaction with peers and others, and model and post pictorially supported vocabulary and sentence frames for her reference. Hold Mee Thaw accountable to produce more language. Teach contextualized vocabulary. Engage her in activities based on (modified) content standards at her linguistically appropriate level as indicated by data.
English Reading/ Writing Levels	Can the student read in the L1? Can the student read in English? What is the student's guided reading level in English? What is the student's grade level in US schools?	This relative newcomer is ready to learn to read in English and will require explicit, targeted reading development that recognizes her maturity, yet engages her in the earliest phases of learning to read and write in English.	Since Mee Thaw is not yet writing at the sentence level in Karen, she is likely to benefit from ongoing oral language development, instruction in letter recognition and formation of Latin script, contextualized vocabulary development, leveled nonfiction books with strong picture support that target her emerging literacy level, and interaction

	Guiding Questions	Student Data	Interpretation
	Is there a difference between the L1 reading level and the English reading level? If so, what actions does this difference call for?		with peers in English. Educators must make it a top priority to develop her reading skills in English, given the brief length of time she has to attend high school.
Exposure to English Outside of School	To what extent does the student interact in English at home? To what extent does the student interact in English before and after school? Does the student have a job that requires using English? Does the student have English-speaking friends outside of school? Does the student live in an enclave community where English is not needed?	Mee Thaw has secured a job at the mall, which will greatly support her oral English language learning, which will in turn support her learning to read and write in English. In addition, she has a circle of friends from the International Club at school that socializes outside of school.	Ensure that all students have internal and external connections that will enhance their oral language and social interactions. Such embedded opportunities for contextualized language development are of critical importance for all ELs. The facts that Mee Thaw is supported by a job where speaking English is required and that she has a social connection where English is spoken are excellent ways to facilitate her language development and confidence.
Standardized Test Data in the Content Areas	Has the student received content instruction in English? What are the English language development levels of the student? Can those levels predict what the student can understand in terms of the standardized assessment questions? What else is evident from these data about this EL, and what cannot be determined? What are the implications for language instruction for this student?	As a newcomer, Mee Thaw receives an exemption for 12 months from taking a standardized Reading assessment, but is required to take the math section. Knowing that she performs at Level 2 in Reading in English, Mee Thaw is unable to derive meaning from grade-level print. As a result, teachers can predict the likelihood of a low score on these assessments due to the English language barrier.	Well-meaning attempts to provide assessments in the first language are not likely to be helpful if there has been no instruction in the L1 and should be avoided, as they are unlikely to result in inaccurate data.

(Continued)

(Continued)

	Guiding Questions	Student Data	Interpretation
Grades/Grade Point Average	Is there a district policy in place for grading ELs? Does the grading policy embody an additive view of ELs? Is the grading policy differentiated based on differentiated language development levels of the EL? Do the grades provide accurate and meaningful information to this student and family? Are the grades based on (modified) content standards? Are report card comments meaningful to this student and family?	Mee Thaw is enrolled in high school, where her teachers are differentiating her content assignments and materials based on her English language development levels. She is performing well within the levels indicated by her data. Her teachers are modifying ninth grade standards for her, implementing differentiated instruction designed to scaffold her learning, and implementing differentiated grading. Mee is earning an A in her social studies class, with a report card notation of "differentiated grading."	Educators can support ELs by providing both accurate and meaningful data through modifying content standards (when needed) and differentiating language demands.
Benchmarks (i.e., incremental levels of achievement within a grade-level that are to be met on the way to mastery of a standard)	Does the district/school embrace the notion that ELs who are placed in a specific grade might not be able to perform at grade-level, due to a variety of factors? Does the district/school recognize the fact that background must be built for ELs who have experienced a lack of opportunity to learn?	At the age of 18, Mee Thaw is older than her grade-level peers, but thanks to her forward-thinking school district administrators, teachers, and stakeholders, Mee Thaw has an opportunity to maximize her high school experience, earn credits, and even to graduate by the end of her 21st year. Her learning has been measured in relation to her own growth.	Administrators and teachers must recognize that Mee Thaw has large gaps in her education that will require consulting the learning progressions in a given subject, backing up to the initial introduction of a concept, and compressing essential learning into meaningful instruction and assessments for her at her current English language development level. This approach will require high quality supplementary materials at her reading level, purposeful daily reading instruction in English targeting her emerging skills, and collaboration among a number of teachers.

106

	Guiding Questions	Student Data	Interpretation
	Does the district/school embrace the fact that a lack of opportunity to learn does not constitute a cognitive deficit or a need for special education, but rather a need for targeted instruction that meets the EL at an appropriate instructional level?	rather than against a superimposed model based on grade-level progressions in which Mee Thaw has not been able to participate.	
Behaviors (e.g., inattentiveness, aggression, inappropriate behavior, withdrawn demeanor, lack of eye contact)	Do all stakeholders operate from an open-minded position that first asks and investigates, rather than judges and stereotypes, when the behaviors of this student are different from those of non-ELs? Have stakeholders received professional development that helps them to interpret any misunderstood behaviors of this student through an EL Lens? Have all stakeholders adopted an orientation of advocacy for this student?	When Mee Thaw appeared at school with an opaque mixture of ground tree bark and water on both sides of her face, curiosity of both staff and students was piqued. Research and inquiry revealed that this cultural cosmetic is applied to enhance beauty. Eventually, Mee Thaw's circle of non-EL friends tried the practice, known as "thanakha."	Districts/schools are reminded to ask questions of cultural brokers in the community before reacting adversely to cultural practices. Positive assumptions support ELs.
Pronunciation/ Accent (e.g., inaccurate sounds, "inappropriate" sounds)	When discussing characteristics of this student, are stakeholders able to identify ethnocentric attitudes and vocabulary that communicate negative perceptions? Are district/school stakeholders committed to setting high expectations for this student?	Mee Thaw's pronunciation in English is predictable, based on a contrastive analysis of sounds in Karen. Her school has incorporated the languages of students into a global studies class that positions ELs as experts to teach useful words and phrases to their classmates, EL and non-EL alike.	Applying the EL Lens informs teachers that terms like *inappropriate sounds*, when applied to EL pronunciation, can be offensive. Rather, when language acquisition is studied, the notion of transference is predictable and common. Educators must learn about basic characteristics of language acquisition to better support ELs.

(Continued)

(Continued)

	Guiding Questions	Student Data	Interpretation
Classroom Performance	Has the EL lived in a culture that encourages competition and outspoken views? Has the EL lived in a culture that promotes success of the group over the success of an individual? Is the EL comfortable asking questions of teachers? Might this EL tend to support others in school work or tests as a means of supporting the group?	Mee Thaw has been socialized in a collectivistic culture which means that her actions must be understood in the context of her whole group. She is unlikely to distinguish herself as an individual by offering answers; she believes it is disrespectful to ask questions of her teacher. Mee Thaw's efforts to assist her peers could possibly be misconstrued as cheating.	Educators must apply the EL Lens before drawing conclusions about Mee Thaw's classroom performance. She might benefit from explicit coaching to assist her in adopting new norms for classroom behavior. Sharing classroom rules of behavior explicitly with students can help reduce misunderstanding.
Information From Parents, Cultural Informants, and Home Visits	Is there a formal structure in place that provides routine communication with this student's parents, both in written forms and also by telephone? Is there a communication center that these parents can call to report absences, check on their student, et cetera, using their first languages? Are these parents consistently involved in school activities through school-based efforts to be welcoming and inclusive? Are there expectations that teachers will conduct home visits and form relationships with parents? Are teachers rewarded for those efforts? Are there enough bilingual associates, tutors, teachers, or outreach workers to meet the needs of this family to the same extent that the needs of non-EL families are met?	Since there is a shortage of Karen interpreters, the school district has hired Mee Thaw's older sister part time to contact Karen-speaking families with school news, to invite them to report school events, to report absences, and to schedule home visits.	Though Mee Thaw's sister is not a university graduate, the district adapted its hiring guidelines to help meet the needs of EL students and families. Districts/schools will benefit from being flexible in order to engage EL families, parents, guardians, et cetera in all aspects of school to the same extent that they communicate with and engage non-EL families, parents, guardians, et cetera.

	Guiding Questions	Student Data	Interpretation
Student Interests	Do teachers infuse this student's interests into instruction to motivate and encourage the student to participate in content learning? If appropriate, is this student positioned to assume the role of expert informant? For example, could this student provide reports that focus on her or his country of origin in social studies class?	Mee Thaw's Karen-speaking expertise has been recognized as she is the "expert" teaching her peers useful words and phrases in her global studies class.	Whenever possible, the expertise and knowledge of ELs should be highlighted, and funds of knowledge brought to the forefront. For example, the social studies department could plan the year's course to include the native countries of the school's ELs. In one such instance, ELs from South Sudan collaborated to research and prepare a presentation to the class on their country and their firsthand experiences.
Other Factors (e.g., giftedness, learning disabilities, physical disabilities)	Has the district/school used means other than standardized assessments to determine whether this student is a candidate for gifted/talented programming? Is there clarity about how this student can be served in such programming?	Soon after her enrollment at high school, Mee Thaw's love of music became apparent. Understanding the value of capitalizing on this interest, her counselor enrolled her in the school chorus and also invited her to try instruments in the band room. Mee Thaw picked up a flute and has continued to play it in the band, thanks to an instrument donation program that aims to provide musical instruments to each student who would like to learn to play one.	Districts/schools should double check the enrollment of ELs in special programs and in extracurricular activities to ensure that they are represented in equitable proportions.

RESOURCE 4.1 Template for Gathering and Interpreting Student Data Using the EL Lens

Student Name: _____

	Guiding Questions	Student Data	Interpretation
Age	Is the student the same age as others in the class? Why or why not? Can placement be appropriately made with approximately same-age peers? Is the student progressing at the same rate as others who are age-level peers in language development?		
Grade	Does the student have academic background built in the first language (L1) that is on grade level?		
Family Background	Is the student living with her or his intact family? If not, what is the situation? What implications might it have on school success?		
Country of Origin, Country of Domicile	Is the country of origin one that suggests the student has experienced trauma, loss, family separation, migration, or other difficult experiences? Has the student lived outside of the country of origin? If so, what are the impacts?		
Immigrant/ Refugee/ Migrant/Other Status	Has the student or family fled for their lives? Might could the family benefit from additional support related to this experience?		
Living Situation (e.g., housing, homelessness)	Does the student have safe housing with a support system of adults?		
Socioeconomic Status (e.g., food security)	When the school week is over and school lunch programs do not operate, does the student have sufficient food? Does the student have material and medical needs met?		
Cultural Background/ Practices	Has the staff been informed of cultural or health practices of this student that they might wonder about?		
Educational Backgrounds	Are the parents of the student literate in their L1? Can the student read in the L1? Is the student on grade level in the L1?		

	Guiding Questions	**Student Data**	**Interpretation**
	Has the student attended school previously? Where? In what grades?		
	Does the student have a transcript that can be translated to afford credit for classes taken?		
First Language/ Script	Does the student's L1 utilize the Latin script, or is another writing system used?		
	What implications does this information have for literacy instruction in English?		
	What implications might exist for handwriting instruction?		
First Language Listening/ Speaking Levels	Can the student interact with others in the L1? Is the EL on par with other ELs of the same age and experience?		
First Language Reading/ Writing Levels	Can the student write his or her name in the L1? A sentence? A paragraph? Can the student read in the L1?		
Length of Time in the United States	How long has the student lived in the United States?		
	Where did the student live before that?		
	What were the living conditions?		
	What has the student experienced in the United States?		
English Listening/ Speaking Levels	Can the student understand simple questions in English?		
	Can the student point to objects or follow simple directions in English?		
	What information does the English language development assessment provide about levels of language?		
English Reading/ Writing Levels	Can the student read in the L1?		
	Can the student read in English?		
	What is the student's guided reading level in English?		
	What is the student's grade level in US schools?		
	Is there a difference between the L1 reading level and the English reading level?		
	If so, what actions does this difference call for?"		

(Continued)

RESOURCE 4.1 (Continued)

	Guiding Questions	Student Data	Interpretation
Exposure to English Outside of School	To what extent does the student interact in English at home? To what extent does the student interact in English before and after school? Does the student have a job that requires using English? Does the student have English-speaking friends outside of school? Does the student live in an enclave community where English is not needed?		
Standardized Test Data in the Content Areas	Has the student received content instruction in English? What are the English language development levels of the student? Can those levels predict what the student can understand in terms of the standardized assessment questions? What else is evident from these data about this EL, and what cannot be determined? What are the implications for language instruction for this student?		
Grades/Grade Point Average	Is there a district policy in place for grading ELs? Does the grading policy embody an additive view of ELs? Is the grading policy differentiated based on differentiated language development levels of the EL? Do the grades provide accurate and meaningful information this student and family? Are the grades based on (modified) content standards? Are report card comments meaningful to this student and family?		
Benchmarks (i.e., incremental levels of achievement within a grade level that are to be met on the way to mastery of a standard)	Does the district/school embrace the notion that ELs who are placed in a specific grade might not be able to perform at grade level due to a variety of factors? Does the district/school recognize that background must be built for ELs who have experienced a lack of opportunity to learn?		

	Guiding Questions	Student Data	Interpretation
	Does the district/school embrace the fact that a lack of opportunity to learn does not constitute a cognitive deficit or a need for special education, but rather a need for targeted instruction that meets the EL at an appropriate instructional level?		
Behaviors (e.g., inattentiveness, aggression, inappropriate behavior, withdrawn demeanor, lack of eye contact)	Do all stakeholders operate from an open-minded position that first asks and investigates, rather than judges and stereotypes, when the behaviors of this student are different from those of non-ELs? Have stakeholders received professional development that helps them to interpret any misunderstood behaviors of this student through an EL Lens? Have all stakeholders adopted an orientation of advocacy for this student?		
Pronunciation/ Accent (e.g., inaccurate sounds, "inappropriate" sounds)	When discussing characteristics of this student, are stakeholders able to identify ethnocentric attitudes and vocabulary that communicate negative perceptions? Are district/school stakeholders committed to setting high expectations for this student?		
Classroom Performance	Has the EL lived in a culture that encourages competition and outspoken views? Has the EL lived in a culture that promotes success of the group over the success of an individual? Is the EL comfortable asking questions of teachers? Might this EL tend to support others in school work or tests as a means of supporting the group?		
Information From Parents, Cultural Informants, and Home Visits	Is there a formal structure in place that provides routine communication with this student's parents, both in written forms and also by telephone? Is there a communication center that these parents can call to report absences, check on their student, et cetera, using their first languages? Are these parents consistently involved in school activities through school-based efforts to be welcoming and		

(Continued)

RESOURCE 4.1 (Continued)

	Guiding Questions	**Student Data**	**Interpretation**
	inclusive? Are there expectations that teachers will conduct home visits and form relationships with these parents? Are teachers rewarded for those efforts? Are there enough bilingual associates, tutors, teachers, or outreach workers to meet the needs of this family to the same extent that the needs of non-EL families are met?		
Student Interests	Do teachers infuse this student's interests into instruction to motivate and encourage the student to participate in content learning? If appropriate, is this student positioned to assume the role of expert informant? For example, could this student provide reports that focus on her or his country of origin in social studies class?		
Other Factors (e.g., giftedness, learning disabilities, physical disabilities)	Has the district/school used means other than standardized assessments to determine whether this student is a candidate for gifted/talented programming? Is there clarity about how this student can be served in such programming?		

FOR FURTHER READING ON DIFFERENT LANGUAGES

Ethnologue: Languages of the World: www.ethnologue.com

Haghighat, C. (2005). *Language profiles* (vols. 1–3). Toronto, ON: World Languages Publishing.

Swan, M., & Smith, B. (Eds.). (2001). *Learner English.* New York, NY: Cambridge University Press.

Align Standards- 5
Based Assessments
and Grading With
ELs' Current Levels
of Linguistic and
Content
Development

If we want grades to be accurate indicators of mastery, then we have to remove any barrier to students coming to know the material, as well as any barrier to their successful demonstrations of mastery. To not do either of these tasks makes any subsequent grades earned false; they are based on misinformation, and the grade is no longer valid or useful.

(Wormeli, 2006, p. 121)

In order to facilitate EL academic achievement, assessments and grading must be aligned with individual students' current levels of English language development/proficiency (ELD/P). Further, these assessments and their associated grades must be reflective of learning opportunities that are both grounded in standards and tied to students' current content instructional levels. Only then will grades accurately reflect what ELs know and can do in the content areas.

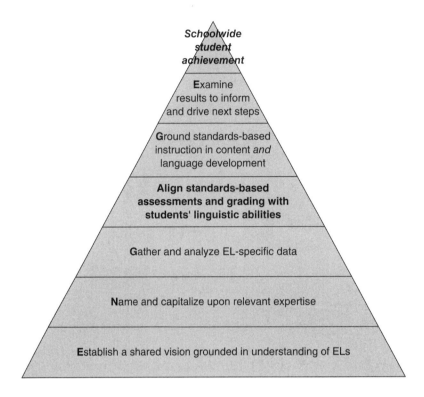

The rationale for beginning discussion of the teaching–learning cycle with detailed discussion of assessment and grading, rather than instruction, is drawn from backward lesson design (BLD) (Wiggins & McTighe, 2006). In this approach, educators

1. determine what students must know and be able to do,

2. identify acceptable evidence for having met those learning targets, and finally,

3. plan instruction.

The implementation of this process and the associated teaching and assessment described in Chapters 5 and 6 is represented in Figure 5.1.

The present chapter discusses the first two steps in the aforementioned BLD approach for ELs. Table 5.1 outlines the steps that administrators, teachers, and other stakeholders must undertake in order to develop and implement EL-specific expectations and associated assessments. This collaborative process will culminate in differentiated assessment and grading. (The third part of the BLD process for ELs, differentiated lesson planning, is described in Chapter 6.)

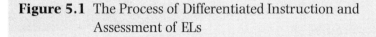

Figure 5.1 The Process of Differentiated Instruction and Assessment of ELs

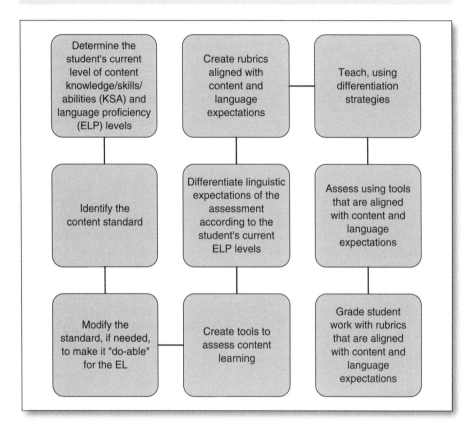

Appropriate assessment and grading of students who are still learning English is a complicated endeavor, since the language demands of many content standards may exceed the ELD/P levels of K–12 ELs. For example kindergarten language arts standards may be overly linguistically demanding, not only for beginning ELs in kindergarten, but also for some ELs in high school. However, by breaking the process of alignment of assessment and grading of ELs into stages, the process becomes clear and "do-able." Table 5.1 lists the detailed series of stages in the alignment process.

Each of these stages in the process of aligning assessments and grading with ELs' current levels of linguistic and content development will be discussed in detail in this chapter, with specific attention given to the responsibilities of administrators, teachers, and other stakeholders in the EL educational process.

Table 5.1 Stages and Areas of Responsibility/Action for Aligning Standards-Based Assessments and Grading With ELs' Current Levels of Linguistic and Content Development

Stages/Areas of Responsibility	Leadership Team Responsibilities	Teacher Responsibilities	Other Stakeholder Responsibilities (e.g., school board members, parents)
1. Setting high expectations	Maintain high expectations for EL achievement.	Enact high expectations for EL achievement.	Advocate on behalf of ELs for reaching high expectations.
2. Implementing collaboration	Establish an environment that facilitates teacher–staff collaboration to support EL achievement.	Collaborate with peers to support EL achievement.	Support and value collaborative efforts and honor collaborative success.
3. Developing/ enhancing knowledge of content standards	Ensure that teachers and other stakeholders understand which content standards must guide teaching, what is included in those standards, and how the standards work through professional development; participate in this professional development.	Take advantage of professional development opportunities related to the content standards to learn which standards must guide teaching, what is included in those standards, and how the standards work.	Learn, through various means, which content standards must guide teaching, what is included in those standards, and how the standards work.
4. Modifying content standards, as needed	Facilitate opportunities for teachers to learn to (1) determine the EL's current level of knowledge, skills, and abilities in the content area; (2) examine the EL's background characteristics and determine implications for content learning; (3) analyze the extent to which the EL can meet a given individual content standard; and	Learn to (1) determine the EL's current level of knowledge, skills, and abilities in the content area; (2) examine the EL's background characteristics and determine implications for content learning; (3) analyze the extent to which the EL can meet a given individual content standard; and	Gain understanding of the need for teachers to (1) determine the EL's current level of knowledge, skills, and abilities in the content area; (2) examine the EL's background characteristics and determine implications for content learning;

Stages/Areas of Responsibility	Leadership Team Responsibilities	Teacher Responsibilities	Other Stakeholder Responsibilities (e.g., school board members, parents)
	(4) determine the next logical "step" on the EL's learning trajectory toward meeting the content standard.	(4) determine the next logical "step" on the EL's learning trajectory toward meeting the content standard.	(3) analyze the extent to which the EL can meet a given individual content standard; (4) determine the next logical "step" on the EL's learning trajectory toward meeting the content standard; and (5) support and widely communicate the value of such modification efforts throughout the community.
5. Developing/enhancing knowledge of ELD/P standards	Ensure that teachers and other stakeholders understand the ELD/P standards that must guide teaching, what is included in those standards, and how the standards work through professional development; participate in this professional development.	Take advantage of professional development opportunities related to the ELD/P standards to learn which standards must guide teaching, what is included in those standards, and how the standards work.	Learn, through various means, which ELD/P standards must guide teaching, what is included in those standards, and how the standards work.
6. Developing knowledge of linguistic differentiation, based on state English language development/proficiency standards	Facilitate opportunities for teachers to learn to differentiate expectations according to ELs' individual English language development levels; participate in this professional development.	Learn to differentiate expectations according to ELs' individual English language development levels.	Gain understanding of the need for teachers to differentiate expectations according to ELs' individual English language development levels. Support and widely communicate such efforts throughout the community.

(Continued)

Table 5.1 (Continued)

Stages/Areas of Responsibility	Leadership Team Responsibilities	Teacher Responsibilities	Other Stakeholder Responsibilities (e.g., school board members, parents)
7. Building knowledge of EL-appropriate assessments	Recognize that one-size-fits-all assessments are unlikely to gather accurate data about ELs, creating the need for more culturally and linguistically accessible assessments. Provide needed professional development on principles of EL-appropriate assessment creation; participate in this professional development. Ensure teachers have the freedom to develop and use assessment tools needed in order to obtain accurate data about what students know and can do.	Distinguish assessments that yield meaningful EL data from those that don't, leading to an understanding of the need for more linguistically accessible assessments. Learn principles of EL-appropriate assessment design.	Internalize the collective district/school understanding that many assessments designed for native speakers of English do not provide accurate information about what these students know and do. Communicate concerns about inaccurate assessment of ELs with community members, supporting the need for more linguistically accessible assessments. Become familiar with and communicate principles of EL-appropriate assessment design.
8. Developing EL-appropriate assessment tools	Set and communicate expectations that such teacher-created assessments will be implemented, and hold teachers accountable for this implementation.	Design and implement assessments that allow students to best demonstrate what they know and can do in the content areas.	Support and advocate for the development and implementation of assessments that reveal accurate data about ELs.
9. Sharing EL-appropriate assessment tools	Acknowledge and reward teachers for their efforts to design, share, and disseminate differentiated assessment tools that result in accurate data.	Highlight successes in designing EL-appropriate assessment tools. Share and disseminate new differentiated assessment tools that will result in more accurate data; develop a repository of teacher-created differentiated assessment tools.	Communicate successes about the development, implementation, and sharing of EL-appropriate assessment tools. Express appreciation and encouragement to administrators and teachers who support or engage in the design, sharing, and dissemination of differentiated assessment tools that result in accurate data.

Stages/Areas of Responsibility	Leadership Team Responsibilities	Teacher Responsibilities	Other Stakeholder Responsibilities (e.g., school board members, parents)
10. Establishing buy-in for differentiated standards-based grading	Establish buy-in for differentiated grading among teachers, other stakeholders, parents, and students. With teachers, parents, and other stakeholders, discuss and develop the district/school rationale for differentiated standards-based grading.	Discuss and develop, along with administrators and other stakeholders, the district/school rationale for differentiated standards-based grading; adhere to the rationale for differentiated standards-based grading.	Discuss and develop, along with administrators and teachers, the district/school rationale for differentiated standards-based grading; widely communicate and support the district/school rationale for differentiated standards-based grading.
11. Developing differentiated standards-based grading policies and practices	Facilitate opportunities for teachers to learn about differentiated standards-based grading; participate in these opportunities.	Take advantage of district/school learning opportunities focused on differentiated standards-based grading.	Widely communicate support for the development of districts/school differentiated standards-based grading.
12. Implementing differentiated standards-based grading policies and practices	Set and communicate school-/district-wide expectations for differentiated standards-based grading policies and practices with teachers, parents, other stakeholders, and students; make necessary adjustments to reporting systems.	Inform students of standards-based grading policies and practices; enact the policies and practices adopted by the district/school.	Stand by administrators and teachers while actively working to support the entire community in understanding the meaning of standards-based grading policies and practices.
13. Engaging in ongoing support for differentiated standards-based assessment and grading	Support teachers in meeting their differentiated standards-based assessment and grading responsibilities through ongoing professional development; participate in this professional development.	Actively participate in professional development opportunities to enhance differentiated standards-based assessment and grading practices.	Gain understanding of the enhancements needed for effective differentiated standards-based assessment and grading, and communicate them with the entire community
14. Refining differentiated standards-based assessment and grading	Set expectations district-/school-wide for the continued refinement of differentiated standards-based assessment and grading.	Refine implementation of standards-based assessment and grading.	Support refinements to differentiated standards-based assessment and grading; communicate them to the entire community.

AREAS OF RESPONSIBILITY/ACTION FOR ALIGNING STANDARDS-BASED ASSESSMENTS AND GRADING

Stage 1: Setting High Expectations

Leadership Team Responsibilities/Actions

Leadership team members set the district/school tone by determining and maintaining high expectations for EL achievement. As a result of the efforts, modeling, and feedback of these leaders, teachers are better positioned and likely to be more motivated to accomplish the district-/school-wide goal of engaging ELs in accessible standards-based instruction.

Teacher Responsibilities/Actions

Fueled by administrator leadership, teachers must share and maintain high expectations for the academic achievement of each EL in every classroom. This means that teachers carefully engage in practices that take into account the cultural and linguistic characteristics of their students, leading to student success through equitable access to standards-based achievement.

Other Stakeholder Responsibilities/Actions

Other stakeholders in the EL educational process must advocate on behalf of ELs in order to support and facilitate their academic achievement. This means that stakeholders facilitate open communication among administrators, teachers, and the community. Further, they must adopt an informed EL-focused perspective that bases decision making on what is best for ELs.

Stage 2: Implementing Collaboration

Leadership Team Responsibilities/Actions

District/school leaders must facilitate an environment that is conducive to collaboration as a means of expanding the overall capacity of staff. Such supports as providing or embedding time dedicated to collaboration, recognizing collaborative efforts of staff around differentiated standards-based grading and assessment, and communicating successes all help to actualize the fully integrated vision that addresses ELs' social and academic needs.

Teacher Responsibilities/Actions

Responding to administrator leadership, teachers must work collaboratively with one another across their respective areas of expertise to develop and refine ways of assessing and grading ELs in a differentiated manner. This kind of collaboration calls for "reciprocal mentoring" (Jones-Vo et al., 2007), in which teachers with different areas of expertise (e.g., a math teacher and an ESL teacher) mentor one another in how to most effectively meet the instructional needs of ELs. Such a rich team-based approach results in EL-appropriate strategies layered with deeper standards-based concept knowledge, facilitating EL academic achievement.

Other Stakeholder Responsibilities/Actions

Informed of the requirements of effective collaboration (e.g., dedicated planning time, administrator guidance and support, the need for appropriate materials), other stakeholders must provide ongoing support (e.g., school board funding allocations, advocacy for common planning times) for this collaboration, which is designed to provide ELs with access to standards-based achievement. Such support is critical to teacher collaboration and opens the way for other stakeholders to value and honor collaborative successes within and across classrooms.

Stage 3: Developing/Enhancing Knowledge of Content Standards

Leadership Team Responsibilities/Actions

In the current standards-based environment, it is the task of district/ school leaders to ensure that teachers and other stakeholders clearly understand and ground their instruction in specific content standards that have been approved for use in the district/school. Leadership team members must be in a position to provide guidance and professional development that empowers teachers to utilize and enact the content and practices embodied in the standards. These leaders must also participate in *all* professional development provided to support the academic achievement of ELs because "a strong focus on professional development for all staff members, including administrators" has been found to be an "element of effective practice for English learners" (Calderón, Slavin, & Sánchez, 2011, p. 109).

Teacher Responsibilities/Actions

Teachers must willingly participate in activities designed to deepen their understanding of the content standards and how they work, on an ongoing basis. Only when teachers understand the content standards and how they work are they positioned to provide standards-based instruction and assessment for ELs.

Other Stakeholder Responsibilities/Actions

Other stakeholders must be informed about the content standards that constitute the basis of instruction and assessment within the district/school and about how those standards are implemented. Informed stakeholders are better positioned to make appropriate decisions related to district/school needs (e.g., funding for materials, staffing).

Stage 4: Modifying Content Standards, as Needed

The process of developing a student-centered assessment informed by EL data is depicted in Figure 5.2. Part A is reviewed in this section, having been addressed in detail in Chapter 4. This section focuses on Part B in of Figure 5.2, while Parts C and D are discussed in Stage 6: Developing Knowledge of Linguistic Differentiation.

Enacting the model represented in Figure 5.2 requires a number of steps. Part A of the model necessitates three steps, while Part B can be addressed in a single step. (Again, the steps involved in enacting Parts C and D will be addressed in an upcoming section.)

Figure 5.2 Model of EL-Appropriate Assessment Design

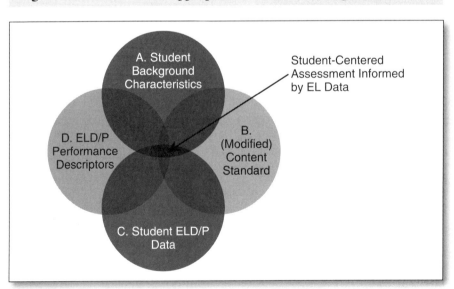

Part A calls for leadership team members, teachers, and other stakeholders to understand how they can work to

1. determine the EL's current level of knowledge, skills, and abilities in the content area;

2. examine the EL's background characteristics and determine implications for content learning; and

3. analyze the extent to which the EL is prepared to meet a given individual content standard;

while Part B requires that teachers

4. determine the next logical step on the EL's learning trajectory toward meeting the content standard.

Tomlinson (2005) reminds educators that "we know that learning happens best when a learning experience pushes the learner a bit beyond his or her independence level" (p. 8). This is true of both language learning and content learning. In a standards-based teaching environment, targeting instruction at students' instructional levels is essential to providing ELs access to standards-based achievement. The three steps composing Part A of Figure 5.2 were addressed in Chapter 4, leaving Part B of Figure 5.2, with its emphasis on modification[1] of content standards, as the focus of this part of the process of aligning standards-based assessment and grading with what ELs currently know and can do. Note that such modification of content standards is carried out only if student data reveal that it is necessary due to differing educational backgrounds or gaps in learning, determined in the data analysis described in Chapter 4.

In the current standards-based instructional environment, many policy makers have asserted the "logic" of requiring that all students at a given grade level meet the same achievement benchmarks. This practice, however, does not take into account the realities of ELs, who enter the grade-level continuum at different points, often with gaps in education and literacy development. In fact, research has revealed that ELs may not follow the same learning trajectory as non-ELs (Linan-Thompson, Cirino, & Vaughn, 2007), and the experiences of many teachers of ELs confirm this.

While some ELs enter US schools on grade level in terms of education and literacy development (in the L1), others arrive in US classrooms without these skills, and their lives may have been complicated by negative or

---

[1]The term *modification* refers to changes to the learning goal (Jung & Guskey, 2012), whereas *accommodations* simply level the playing field (e.g., supports such as extra time).

even traumatic experiences that impact learning (e.g., crossing multiple borders while separated from family members, experiencing war first-hand). Scholars on the topic of standards-based assessment and grading assert that modification of content standards, in order to facilitate student learning and achievement, is not only permissible, but, at times, essential; Jung and Guskey (2012) call for a team approach to this modification process, when student data necessitates it. By modifying content standards, teachers can provide students access to standards-based achievement by starting at an accessible and logical entry point "a bit beyond his or her independence level" (Tomlinson, 2005, p. 8).

Note that such modification of standards, rather than a watered-down approach to instruction, represents the means for scaffolding students to grade-level achievement by supporting them in the step-by-step process of meeting grade-level standards while simultaneously acquiring a new language. Modifying standards and benchmarks so they align with ELs' current levels of both English language development and content understanding is entirely acceptable, recommended, and, in fact, sometimes necessary in order to teach ELs at their current instructional levels. As Jung and Guskey articulate, "a 9th grade English language learner's ELL plan may call for 7th grade vocabulary standards rather than 9th grade standards" (2010, p. 34). In addition, the content requirements of the given standard may need to be modified to align them with the student's current capabilities in the content area, particularly if students have gaps in their education.

Determining *next logical steps* for building on a given student's independence level (Part B in Figure 5.2) may be facilitated by making use of learning progressions (e.g., Next Generation Science Standards, 2013) or other resources. The modification of content standards, when indicated by data, exemplifies student-centered data-based decision making at its finest, supported by federal mandates requiring linguistically accessible learning opportunities for ELs (e.g., *Lau v. Nichols*, 1974).

Leadership team, teacher, and other stakeholder responsibilities for enacting the modification of content standards are discussed next.

Leadership Responsibilities/Actions

In order to appropriately guide and support teachers in the modification of content standards for ELs, district/school leaders must provide teachers with opportunities to learn to implement the four steps involved in Parts A and B of Figure 5.2. Such learning opportunities, focused on analysis of EL-specific data (outlined in Chapter 4) and determination of next logical steps for instruction, may take the following forms:

- Data days
- Professional learning communities
- Grade-level or content-area collaborative meetings (e.g., during common planning times)
- Reciprocal mentoring
- Professional development workshops with embedded time for implementing the four steps

Whichever format administrators choose to facilitate the data-driven modification of content standards, the use of a simple template that integrates information about the student with the content standards (such as the one shown in Table 5.2 and at the end of the chapter in Resource 5.2) can facilitate this process, resulting in an appropriate and accessible modified content standard.

The following example is presented to administrators to clarify steps needed to modify a content standard for an individual EL. This process can be carried out in the collaborative format deemed appropriate (e.g., PLCs) by the administrator.

Example of EL-Specific Content Standard Modification

This example will focus on the differentiation of an English/language arts assessment for Vincente, the seventh-grade EL from Mexico who was described in detail in Chapter 2. Vincente's background characteristics serve as the basis for the modification of content standards as a means to provide him access to standards-based achievement. Previously collected (as described in Chapter 4), they are as shown in Table 5.3.

Based on Vincente's background characteristics and EL-specific data, it is clear that grade-level content standards for reading informational

Table 5.2 Template for Developing Modified Content Standards for ELs

Student Name:			
Current level of knowledge, skills, and abilities in the content area and implications for learning	*Key background characteristics and implications for learning*	*Extent to which the student is prepared to meet the content standard*	*Next logical step: A modified content standard* (refer to learning progressions or other relevant resources for guidance)
Gleaned from data analysis outlined in Chapter 4	Gleaned from data analysis outlined in Chapter 4	Gleaned from data analysis outlined in Chapter 4	Determined through: the use of learning progressions or other resources that reveal the scope and sequence of student learning in the given content area key student background information

Table 5.3 Vincente's Background Characteristics

Background Characteristics	*Vincente*
Age	12
Grade	7
Family Background	Came to United States with single uncle, elderly grandmother, aunt and uncle with two cousins
Country of Origin/Country of Domicile	Mexico
Immigrant/Refugee/Migrant/Other Status	Immigrant
Living Situation (e.g., housing, homelessness)	Small house in a neighborhood inhabited entirely by Mexican and Central American immigrants
Socioeconomic Status (e.g., food security)	Middle socioeconomic status; family members support each other by pooling resources
Cultural Background/Practices	Collectivistic
Educational Background/Content Knowledge, Skills, and Abilities	Missed three years of school in Mexico (as reported by his uncle)
First Language/Script	Spanish, Roman script
First Language Listening/Speaking Levels	Social language appropriate for a seventh grader in Spanish (academic language is well below grade level) (determined by intake assessment in Spanish)
First Language Reading/Writing Levels	Second grade (determined by intake assessment in Spanish)
Length of Time in the United States	One month
English Listening/Speaking Levels	Level 1 in both
English Reading/Writing Levels	Level 1 in both
Exposure to English Outside of School	TV only (lives in enclave community where English is not needed)
Other Factors (e.g., gifted/ talented, special education, physical disabilities)	Just wants to go back to Mexico; lacking motivation to learn English, as he can speak Spanish at home (and even at school); totally disengaged from school; has been taken to the principal for fighting in the cafeteria and throwing a dictionary
Student Interests	His love for soccer and the opportunity to play in his neighborhood motivate him

text are currently out of reach. Specifically, his reading in Spanish has been identified at the second-grade level. In English, Vincente does not read at all. As a result, the seventh-grade content standards must be modified to facilitate his participation in the learning process and to bridge the gap between his current instructional level and the grade-level standards. Only by modifying the seventh-grade standards for reading informational text can teachers provide Vincente with access to meaningful instruction, setting him on track to eventually reach grade level and beyond (see Table 5.4).

As mentioned above, learning progressions can provide teachers with useful guidance regarding the modification of grade-level standards for ELs, when needed. In Vincente's case, his seventh-grade teacher may be

Table 5.4 Analysis of Vincente's Current Instructional Level in English/ Language Arts

Student: Vincente			
Current level of knowledge, skills, and abilities in the content area and implications for learning	*Key background characteristics and implications for learning*	*Extent to which the student is prepared to meet the content standard*	*Next logical step: A modified content standard (refer to learning progressions or other relevant resources for guidance)*
• Below grade level—missed three years of school in Mexico (clearly not at grade level in any subject in Spanish) • Reads at second-grade level in Spanish (will be able to transfer basic concepts of print and other early literacy skills learned in Spanish to reading in English; further reading instruction in Spanish would support his literacy development in English) • Does not read at all in English (needs intensive, explicit instruction in how to read in English [not remediation designed for native speakers of English])	• Does not want to be in the United States—misses his family back in Mexico (unlikely to engage in classroom learning) • Lives in an enclave community (no need for English outside of the school day) • Totally disengaged from school (cannot be expected to do homework; needs relevant and meaningful classroom activities tailored to his interests to draw him out)	• Given the significant gap in his education and his lack of motivation and engagement, Vincente is currently unable to meet the seventh-grade content standard in English/ language arts	

wondering where to begin; a learning progression can clarify instructional next steps. An example of the use of such a learning progression, focused on the reading of informational text, follows.

The learning progression used in this example is organized in seven strands aligned with the Common Core State Standards for English/language arts: four for reading and three for writing. The strand that focuses on the reading of informational text is Strand 4: Reading Informational Texts/Making Meaning at the Text Level (Hess, 2011, p. 5). The essential learning for this strand across all grades is, "Reading is making meaning at the text level and understanding the unique genre features, text structures, and purposes of print and non-print informational texts" (Hess, 2011, p. 32). Within this strand, the Learning Target for the fifth- through eighth- grade span is defined as follows:

> Use content knowledge, knowledge of expository text structures (e.g., compare–contrast, cause–effect, proposition–support, critique), and genre-specific features, to read, comprehend, and analyze a range of informational texts, including textbooks and online texts: Explain, compare, and analyze concepts, events, central ideas, point of view, relevant details." (Hess, 2011, p. 32)

The Learning Target in this learning progression is further broken down into Progress Indicators. In seventh grade, one of the Progress Indicators that Vincente is anticipated to accomplish is "comparing or integrating information from multiple sources to develop deeper understanding of the concept/topic/subject, and resolving conflicting information" (Hess, 2011, p. 32). However, given his current levels of Spanish and English reading proficiency, these are unreasonable expectations; Vincente's ability to achieve this Progress Indicator has not been facilitated through instruction.

The beauty of learning progressions is that they provide teachers with concrete ideas for moving the student forward toward grade-level standards in a developmentally appropriate approach within the given content area. As such, they can serve as a "menu" for teachers to draw from in designing student-centered data-driven instruction. The example learning progression used herein "should be thought of as a general map for learning, not a single route to a final destination" (Hess, 2011, p. 8). Teachers can backtrack from current grade-level expectations to those at lower grade levels until they reach the progress indicator that matches the student's instructional needs. In this case, examination of the progress indicators for combining information from multiple sources revealed the following expectations (Hess, 2011, p. 32):

- Grades 5–6: determining relevance or comparability of concepts and supporting details from multiple sources and integrating them to research a topic
- Grades 3–4: using a variety of sources to research a topic; determining relevance of information; making connections within or across texts
- Grades K–2: making connections among pieces of information (e.g., sequence events, steps in a process, cause–effect, compare–contrast relationships)

Since even the K–2 expectations for combining information from multiple resources are beyond Vincente's current reach, the K–2 progress indicators must be fully explored to ascertain the instructional starting point that will move Vincente toward eventual grade-level achievement. A reasonable starting point for this seventh-grade student might be: "demonstrating basic concepts of print (e.g., follows words/ pictures left-right, top-bottom; matches spoken words to print words; distinguishes words from sentences; book parts)" *in English* from the K–2 progress indicators (Hess, 2011, p. 32).

Such modification is not to be confused with "watering down the curriculum" or "dumbing down instruction." Rather, it is data-based decision making (based on the individual student's background characteristics and EL-specific data); without it, the student would be excluded from meaningful learning opportunities and, ultimately, unable to reach his potential. With the increasing number of ELs entering US schools at older ages and higher grades, it is incumbent upon districts/schools to have an immediate fallback plan for providing each student access to standards-based achievement at her or his individual instructional level.

Teacher Responsibilities/Actions

In their work with ELs, teachers must establish an ongoing focus on students' current levels of knowledge, skills, and abilities. Within the content areas, teachers are encouraged to use all meaningful data that is available to them (e.g., information in the student's cumulative folder, teacher-created assessments that use innovative formats [discussed in Stage 8 below]). Such data will inform the logical next steps in order to move ELs along content learning trajectories, informed by learning progressions or other relevant resources. Based on clear and comprehensive knowledge of content standards (discussed in Stage 3 above) and on student background characteristics (discussed in detail in Chapter 4 and

Table 5.5 Determination of the Next Logical Step for Vincente's Content Learning

Student: Vincente			
Current level of knowledge, skills, and abilities in the content area and implications for learning	*Key background characteristics and implications for learning*	*Extent to which the student is prepared to meet the content standard*	*Next logical step: A modified content standard* (refer to learning progressions or other relevant resources for guidance)
• Below grade level—missed three years of school in Mexico (clearly not at grade level in any subject in Spanish) • Reads at second-grade level in Spanish (will be able to transfer basic concepts of print and other early literacy skills learned in Spanish to reading in English; further reading instruction in Spanish would support his literacy development in English) • Does not read at all in English (needs intensive, explicit instruction in how to read in English [not remediation designed for native speakers of English])	• Does not want to be in the United States—misses his family back in Mexico (unlikely to engage in classroom learning) • Lives in an enclave community (no need for English outside of the school day) • Totally disengaged from school (cannot be expected to do homework; needs relevant and meaningful classroom activities tailored to his interests to draw him out)	• Given the significant gap in his education and his lack of motivation and engagement, Vincente is currently unable to meet the seventh-grade content standard in English/language arts	• "demonstrating basic concepts of print (e.g., follows words/pictures left-right, top-bottom; matches spoken words to print words; distinguishes words from sentences; book parts)" in English

mentioned above in this stage), teachers can envision and plan ways to *incrementally* bridge the gap from what ELs currently know and can do in the content areas to grade-level expectations[2].

---

[2]Note that this content gap may not be bridged in the course of a single year. For example, ELs in high school will not have studied American history throughout their educational careers; situations such as this require the building of significant background in order for ELs to meet grade-level standards.

Other Stakeholder Responsibilities/Actions

After gaining understanding of the rationale for and steps involved in the content standard modification process, other stakeholders must assume district-/school-wide supportive roles by widely communicating the value of such modification efforts. In this way, these stakeholders actively participate in the essential charge to provide ELs access to standards.

Stage 5: Developing/Enhancing Knowledge of ELD/P Standards

Leadership Team Responsibilities/Actions

Grounded in the guiding principle that all teachers are teachers of language, it is essential that leadership teams provide opportunities for teachers to learn what the approved ELD/P standards are and how the ELD/P standards can be integrated into their content instruction. Such professional development empowers teachers to facilitate the simultaneous learning of content and language across the curriculum and to scaffold students through the necessary progression toward language proficiency. In the same way that leadership teams must participate in professional development around content standards, these district/school leaders must become knowledgeable about ELD/P standards in order to lead their implementation.

Teacher Responsibilities/Actions

Given that all teachers are teachers of language, it is their responsibility to take full advantage of professional development opportunities related to ELD/P standards, leading ultimately to increased EL achievement.

Other Stakeholder Responsibilities/Actions

As part of their work to promote clarity and singularity of vision, other stakeholders must become informed about the ELD/P standards and their implementation within the district/school. Thus informed, these stakeholders are better positioned to engage with the community to provide accurate information about the concrete steps that the district/school is taking to increase EL achievement.

Stage 6: Developing Knowledge of Linguistic Differentiation

Leadership Team Responsibilities/Actions

Guided by the vision for meeting the academic needs of ELs, leadership teams must facilitate teacher learning in the process of differentiating EL expectations according to their individual English language development levels. These professional development opportunities must be tied to the ELD/P standards approved at the state level and in use in local contexts. These professional development sessions should address

1. fundamentals of the second language acquisition process
2. ELD/P score performance descriptors at each level and in each domain (listening, speaking, reading, and writing)
3. knowledge of how to align language demands of assessments to ELs' ELD/P levels in order to create linguistically differentiated assessments
   a. Analyzing assessments for language demands, while considering the types of language that the student can understand and produce
   b. Recognizing the value and essential nature of visual support in assessment

The following subsections discuss the details to be included in these professional development sessions.

Professional Development on Fundamentals of the Second Language Acquisition Process

Researchers in second language acquisition agree that the development of English proficiency is an incremental process that follows predictable stages over time. The process of learning English is impacted by the language(s) that the individual already knows, such that the process is easier and quicker for those who already know a language similar to English (e.g., Swedish) and more difficult for those whose first language is more distant from English (e.g., Japanese). One important aspect of the impact of language distance is the script in which it is written. It can be anticipated that a student who writes in the Latin script (e.g., in Spanish), can more easily transfer writing skills to English than a student who writes using characters (e.g., in Mandarin). Teacher-friendly volumes that address principles of second language acquisition can serve as vital resources for these professional development activities (e.g., Freeman & Freeman, 2004; TESOL, 2006a).

English Language Development/Proficiency Score Performance Descriptors at Each Level and in Each Domain (Listening, Speaking, Reading, and Writing)

First and foremost, educators must realize that ELs' levels of ELD/P are not matched with their grade levels. That is, students at any level of ELD/P can appear in any grade level (e.g., Level 1 high school students, Level 5 kindergarteners). Against the backdrop of this understanding, teachers can clearly focus their attention on the individual ELD/P levels of their students in each language domain.

While states utilize various ELD/P assessments, all of these tests result in scores that indicate ELs' levels of listening, speaking, reading, and writing and, often, a composite (or overall) score. Generally, these scores range from 1 (the lowest level) to 5 (the highest level). A designation of "6" may be used for ELs who have been deemed to be proficient in English (e.g., as is the practice in the WIDA Consortium, a group of more than 35 states working together to meet the needs of ELs).

The performance descriptors that match the various levels of ELD/P serve as the cornerstone for linguistic differentiation. As such, the performance descriptors for each ELD/P level serve as an essential reference point for data-based decision making when providing ELs with access to achievement based on content standards. As an example, the Teachers of English to Speakers of Other Languages performance descriptors for English language proficiency levels 1–5 are listed in Table 5.6.

Understanding what ELs at each ELD/P level know and can do in English provides teachers with an understanding of how to ensure that their assessments are accessible to ELs, resulting in accurate data about what those students know and can do in the content areas.

Knowledge of How to Align Language Demands of Assessments to ELs' ELD/P Levels in Order to Create Linguistically Differentiated Assessments

Once teachers know what ELs know and can do in English, based on the performance descriptors associated with their ELD/P test scores, they are positioned to design targeted assessments that allow ELs to demonstrate what they know and can do in the content areas given their current abilities to express understanding in English. The process of matching the language demands of the assessment to the ELD/P level of the individual student requires that teachers analyze assessments for their language demands while considering the types of language that the student can understand and produce, and that teachers recognize the importance of visual support in the assessment of ELs. First, we examine the process of analyzing assessments for their language demands.

Analyzing Assessments for Language Demands

In order to obtain an accurate reflection of what ELs know and can do using standards-based assessments, teachers must adopt the perspective of the EL who is described by test data. For example, if the student is described as performing at Level 3 in both reading and writing, by definition, this

Table 5.6 Performance Descriptors for TESOL's Five Levels of English Language Proficiency

Level 1–Starting

At L1, students initially have limited or no understanding of English. They rarely use English for communication. They respond nonverbally to simple commands, statements, and questions. As their oral comprehension increases, they begin to imitate the verbalizations of others by using single words or simple phrases, and they begin to use English spontaneously.

At the earliest stage, these learners construct meaning from text primarily through illustrations, graphs, maps, and tables.

Level 2–Emerging

At L2, students can understand phrases and short sentences. They can communicate limited information in simple everyday and routine situations by using memorized phrases, groups of words, and formulae. They can use selected simple structures correctly, but still systematically produce basic errors. Students begin to use general academic vocabulary and familiar everyday expressions. Errors in writing are present that often hinder communication.

Level 3–Developing

At L3, students understand more complex speech but still may require some repetition. They use English spontaneously but may have difficulty expressing all their thoughts due to a restricted vocabulary and a limited command of language structure. Students at this level speak in simple sentences, which are comprehensible and appropriate, but which are frequently marked by grammatical errors. Proficiency in reading may vary considerably. Students are most successful constructing meaning from texts for which they have background knowledge upon which to build.

Level 4–Expanding

At L4, students' language skills are adequate for most day-to-day communication needs. They communicate in English in new or unfamiliar settings but have occasional difficulty with complex structures and abstract academic concepts. Students at this level may read with considerable fluency and are able to locate and identify the specific facts within the text. However, they may not understand texts in which the concepts are presented in a decontextualized manner, the sentence structure is complex, or the vocabulary is abstract or has multiple meanings. They can read independently, but may have occasional comprehension problems, especially when processing grade-level information.

Level 5–Bridging

At L5, students can express themselves fluently and spontaneously on a wide range of personal, general, academic, or social topics in a variety of contexts. They are poised to function in an environment with native speaking peers with minimal language support or guidance.

Students have a good command of technical and academic vocabulary as well of idiomatic expressions and colloquialisms. They can produce clear, smoothly flowing, well-structured texts of differing lengths and degrees of linguistic complexity. Errors are minimal, difficult to spot, and generally corrected when they occur.

Source: TESOL, 2006b (used with permission).

student can manage to write in simple sentences and some complex sentences as well. Therefore, the design of the standards-based assessment for this student should incorporate reading accessible to Level 3 students that elicits a level of writing commensurate with ELD/P data[3]. By matching the linguistic demands of the assessment to the current linguistic abilities of the student, teachers afford ELs the opportunity to demonstrate what they know and can do. In so doing, teachers provide ELs with a basic civil right: access to standards-based achievement.

For ELs, assessment language must be analyzed at the word level, the sentence level, and the discourse (extended expression) level. This process helps teachers discern what types of text are appropriate for specific students, as indicated by their ELD/P levels. Table 5.7 provides general guidance about the types of language that are accessible to ELs at the various ELD/P levels.

The analysis of the language demands of assessments may reveal to teachers that their assessments include unnecessarily difficult language that precludes ELs from demonstrating what they know and can do in the given content area. Such unnecessary linguistic barriers result in inaccurate test data, as students cannot perform to their best ability on tests that they cannot fully understand and/or that require language production that is beyond their capabilities. The general rule is this: Teachers must use pretaught language that is accessible to ELs when assessing what the ELs know and can do.

When analyzing language at the word level, teachers must be aware that some commonly used vocabulary classification systems designed for non-ELs are not necessarily applicable for ELs. For example, the three

Table 5.7 General Guidance About Types of Language Accessible to ELs at Different ELD/P Levels

	Word Level	**Sentence Level**	**Discourse Level**
Level 1	X		
Level 2	X	X	
Level 3	X	X	X
Level 4	X	X	X
Level 5	X	X	X

[3]The exception to this guidance is the assessment of English/language arts; when assessing language, teachers should not necessarily match test language to the ELs' level of ELD/P.

tiers described by Isabel Beck, Margaret McKeown, and Linda Kucan (2002) were defined with reference to "a mature literate individual's vocabulary" (p. 8). These authors state that Tier 1 words, "the most basic words—*clock, baby, happy, walk* . . . rarely require instructional attention." Of course, these words do, in fact, require instructional attention for ELs, leaving this three-tiered system of vocabulary categorization mismatched in its meaningfulness for ELs.

EL-specific taxonomies for language analysis provide far more meaningful insight into EL vocabulary development. For example, the WIDA Consortium offers several conceptualizations of language development (e.g., WIDA, n.d.a; WIDA, n.d.b; WIDA n.d.c), starting at (or even before) the word level and including the sentence and discourse levels. This type of EL-specific notion of language development provides more authentic utility for teachers working to analyze the linguistic demands of their assessments. This EL-specific approach facilitates analysis of the various features of language at all three levels (word, sentence, and discourse). It also recognizes that ELs bring linguistic resources to the classroom that are not the same as those of non-ELs. As a result, expectations for ELs can be guided by the normal trajectory that they follow in learning language in school (in contrast to "the mature literate individual's vocabulary" [Beck, McKeown, & Kucan, 2002, p. 8]).

Common errors in assessment development at the word level include the following:

- Unnecessarily difficult vocabulary
- Use of untaught vocabulary (vocabulary must have been taught to the student, even in another class)

Analysis of assessment language at the word level involves consideration of the following questions:

- Is the included vocabulary essential to the standard?
- Has instruction and use of the word/phrase been explicit and frequent for ELs, with appropriate scaffolding and support (e.g., pictures, models, demonstrations, video clips, peer interaction)?
- Has the use of the word/phrase been contextualized for ELs (both within instruction and within assessment)?
- Is there evidence (in written, spoken, or nonverbal form) that the EL(s) who will take the test know(s) the word/phrase?

If the answer to all of these questions is "yes," the words in the assessment are appropriate for use. Likewise, at the word level, these questions can be used to inform the creation of an EL-appropriate differentiated assessment.

When analyzing language at the sentence level, teachers must recognize that ELs gradually develop the ability to understand and produce sentences of increasing length and complexity. As a result, sentences that are accessible to ELs at higher levels of ELD/P may be incomprehensible to ELs at lower levels of ELD/P, even though ELs at lower levels may very well grasp the associated content or essential learning. When assessing ELs at lower levels of ELD/P, the most accurate results will be obtained through matching the language of the test to the language level of the student.

Common sentence-level errors in the development of assessments include the following:

- Use of passive voice (e.g., "the experiment was conducted by the teacher" rather than the preferred active voice, as in "the teacher conducted the experiment")
- Unnecessarily complicated verb tenses
- Unnecessarily complex constructions

Teachers must consider the following questions in the analysis of sentence-level language within an assessment:

- Is the length of the sentences used in the assessment appropriate to the ELD/P level of the student(s) who will take the test?
- Are the academic language constructions (e.g., "Contrary to popular belief," "The greater the mass, the greater the force . . .") that are used in the sentences known by the EL(s) who will take the test?
- Have the tenses used throughout the assessment been mastered by the EL(s) who will take the test (e.g., simple present tense [I go], simple past [I went]), as opposed to overly complicated tenses (e.g., past perfect [I had gone], future perfect [I will have gone])?
- Is the complexity of the sentences used in the assessment appropriate for the EL(s) who will take the test?
  - simple = subject + verb (appropriate for students at TESOL Level 2 [cited above] and beyond)
    - Example: The number of ELs in the United States is increasing.
  - compound = subject + verb + connecting word (e.g., *and, but, or, yet*) + subject + verb (often appropriate for students at the upper range of TESOL Level 3 [cited above] and beyond)
    - Example: The number of ELs in the United States is increasing, but the number of teachers with ESL/bilingual endorsements is not keeping pace.

- o complex = subject + verb + *who . . . , that . . . , which . . . , so . . . , although . . . , because . . . ,* et cetera) (often appropriate for students at the upper range of TESOL Level 4 [cited above] and beyond)
  - Example: Although Spanish is the widely spoken first language among ELs, there are over 100 additional language groups represented in US schools.
- o compound–complex = compound sentence + at least one dependent clause (appropriate for students at TESOL Level 5 [cited above] and beyond)
  - Example: The number of immigrant ELs continues to grow, and the number of refugee ELs in US classrooms continues to diversify, so the need for more skilled educators of ELs is projected well into the future.

If the answer to all of these questions when analyzing the sentence level is "yes," the sentences in the assessment are appropriate for use. Likewise, at the sentence level, these questions can be used to inform the determination of linguistic expectations of ELs when creating an EL-appropriate differentiated assessment.

Common errors at the discourse level when creating assessments include the following:

- Potentially unclear or misleading questions (e.g., a question with the phrase "all of these except," where the word *except* has not been taught and/or is not highlighted)
- Use of "test language" (e.g., "all of the following . . ." rather than "all of these . . .")

When analyzing assessments at the discourse (extended expression) level, teachers consider the following questions:

- Is the organization of the discourse (e.g., paragraph, essay, lab report) accessible to the ELs who will complete the assessment?
- Is the length of the discourse aligned with the linguistic stamina of the EL(s) who will complete the assessment?
- Is the variety of sentence types comprehensible to and appropriate for the EL(s) who will complete the assessment?
- Is the language used to connect and transition between ideas in the text comprehensible to the EL(s) who will complete the assessment?
- Has the discourse-level language of the assessment been explicitly taught to ELs in meaningful ways?
- Have students been held accountable in class for using the discourse-level language of the assessment?

If the answer to all of these questions when analyzing the discourse level is "yes," the sentences in the assessment are appropriate for use. Likewise, at the discourse level, these questions can be used to inform the determination of linguistic expectations of ELs when creating an EL-appropriate differentiated assessment.

The aim of these recommendations is to reduce the language demands of content tests to the extent possible. Simplifying language on tests allows teachers to disentangle and independently evaluate two separate and distinct constructs: content understanding and English skills. As such, ELs' content test scores represent more accurate achievement data.

Example of Assessment Language Analysis

Given that Vincente's data reveals that seventh-grade reading standards are inappropriate for him, teachers must develop assessments aligned with the modified standards upon which they are basing instruction. The questions above (and those listed in Resource 5.1) can serve as a checklist for the development of this tool.

To assess Vincente's capabilities in "demonstrating basic concepts of print (e.g., follows words/pictures left-right, top-bottom; matches spoken words to print words; distinguishes words from sentences; book parts)" *in English* from the K–2 progress indicators (Hess, 2011, p. 32), an assessment that combines simple verbal responses as well as nonverbal ones is recommended. Vincente can demonstrate his understanding through answering questions such as the following:

- Is this a word or a picture? (teacher points to a picture)
- Do you start reading at the left or the right side of the page? (teacher points to both sides of the page while stating the question)
- Do you start at the top or the bottom? (teacher points to the top and bottom of the page while stating the question)
- Is this a word or a sentence? (teacher points to a word, circling it with a finger)
- Is this a page or the cover? (teacher points to a page)

The following questions could elicit nonverbal responses:

- Show me a picture.
- Which word is *pencil?* (teacher presents several words to the student, who points to the correct word)
- Show me the cover of the book.
- Point to the back of the book.

Since these assessment questions are nonverbal (and represent pre-taught vocabulary), they meet the threshold of acceptability for a Level 1 EL, based on the word-level language analysis questions (see Table 5.8).

Determining how the student will be assessed *prior* to developing the lesson plans is the means by which teachers ensure that their instruction facilitates the desired outcome.

Recognizing the Value and Essential Nature of Visual Support in Assessment

The value of visual support in assessing second language learners was recognized over three decades ago (Omaggio, 1979), while more recent researchers also suggest that these supports be offered to ELs during assessment (e.g., Butler & Stevens, 1997; Kopriva, 2000). Teachers of English to Speakers of Other Languages (TESOL) is clear in its recommendation that ELs at Levels 1–4 be provided with instructional supports, including visual, graphic, and interactive supports (TESOL, 2009, p. 73).

Example of Inclusion of Visual Support in Assessment

All of the example questions above demonstrate the use of visual support in assessment (e.g., pointing to a picture, handling a real book, gesturing to a word) that is matched to the student's current linguistic ability while focus is maintained on the appropriate content standard.

In the context of all of these professional development initiatives, administrators must participate fully in order to facilitate and support collaborative efforts among teachers eager to reconceptualize current assessments or design new assessments appropriate for ELs at varying levels of ELD/P. This essential work may be accomplished by remunerating teachers willing to take on such tasks after school or over the summer.

Table 5.8 Example Assessment Analysis at the Word Level

Word Level		
1. Is the included vocabulary essential to the standard?	__X_ yes	___ no
2. Has instruction and use of the word/phrase been explicit and frequent for ELs, with appropriate scaffolding and support (e.g., pictures, models, demonstrations, video clips, peer interaction)?	__X_ yes	___ no
3. Has the use of the word/phrase been contextualized for ELs (both within instruction and within assessment)?	__X_ yes	___ no
4. Is there evidence (in written, spoken, or nonverbal form) that the EL(s) who will take the test know(s) the word/phrase?	__X_ yes	___ no

Teacher Responsibilities/Actions

Teachers must learn to differentiate expectations according to ELs' individual English language development levels. This means that they implement each aspect of the professional development led by their administrators (described in detail above), which focuses on the following topics:

1. Basic characteristics of the second language acquisition process

2. ELD/P score performance descriptors at each level (listening, speaking, reading, and writing)

3. Knowledge of how to use language demands to create linguistically differentiated assessment
   a. Analyzing assessments for language demands
   b. Recognizing the value and essential nature of visual support in assessment

Teachers are encouraged to make the linguistic differentiation process do-able in their contexts by starting small. For instance, a teacher might focus attention on a single unit of instruction that has historically been difficult to teach through the lens of a specific EL. Another approach could be the collaborative revision of key assessments used throughout the school year by a given grade-level or content-area team. Such work can be accomplished in PLCs or possibly over the summer.

Other Stakeholder Responsibilities/Actions

The process of differentiating assessments according to ELs' individual ELD/P levels represents a major paradigm shift in district/school practice. This process must be understood by other stakeholders to the extent that they can justify and defend it. These stakeholders are tasked with supporting and communicating the process throughout the community, as well as sharing positive outcomes in EL achievement, grounded in and reflected by data.

Stage 7: Building Knowledge of EL-Appropriate Assessments

Leadership Team Responsibilities/Actions

In order to get accurate data about what ELs know and can do, districts/schools must remove barriers to student demonstration of learning. Wormeli (2006, p. 121) asserts that "barriers in . . . assessment include inappropriate testing formats . . . [and] using the same tools with all students when different tools are needed by some." Leaders at the district/school level must recognize and acknowledge the fact that most, if not all, one-size-fits-all assessments are unlikely to result in accurate data about what ELs know and can do. These leaders are then positioned to facilitate and participate in professional development that enriches teacher knowledge of the fundamentals of EL-appropriate assessment development. Against this backdrop, leaders must then afford teachers the freedom to develop new assessments or modify existing ones, resulting in tools that are culturally and linguistically appropriate. Only in the context of this type of culturally and linguistically responsive environment can teachers implement assessments that are differentiated to be appropriate for the students that they serve.

Teacher professional development focused on how to create EL-appropriate assessment integrates four separate components (see Figure 5.2).

1. Student background characteristics (e.g., reading level in English, educational background) (addressed in Chapter 4)

2. Modified content standards as defined or differentiated within the curriculum (addressed above in Stage 4)

3. Student ELD/P data (addressed in Stage 6 above)

4. Associated standards-based ELD/P performance descriptors (addressed in Stage 6 above)

When teachers integrate all of these factors into assessment design, the resulting tool can reveal accurate information about what the EL knows and can do in the given content area, since both the language and the content have been differentiated, allowing the student to engage at her or his data-informed level.

Particularly for students at the lower levels of ELD/P, administrators and teachers must ensure that assessments also engage these students in higher order thinking (e.g., application, analysis, synthesis, evaluation, creation). While students at Levels 1–3 are limited in their ability to express content knowledge in English, they are, nevertheless, fully capable of engaging in such levels of thought. As a result, teachers who wish to elicit such thinking must empower their students to express their thoughts with appropriate scaffolds embedded in the assessment process. These scaffolds may be associated with representation and/or elicitation. Representative scaffolds support language learning by depicting or showing concepts and making their relationships visible or evident. Other necessary scaffolds that teachers must utilize are those designed to elicit English language production, both orally and in writing. Utilizing both essential types of scaffold ensures that ELs advance both in their content knowledge, skills, and abilities, and in their development of English language proficiency. Examples of each type of essential scaffold are presented in Table 5.9.

At times, these two types of scaffolds can be merged, as in labeled photographs or graphic organizers that include sentence starters.

Teachers must integrate these essential scaffolds in order to design appropriate assessments for ELs. The purposeful use of the same scaffolds in both instruction and assessment constitutes best practice. Following is a list of assessment products and performances tailored to each TESOL ELD/P level. These examples incorporate suggested scaffolds but are meant to prompt teachers' thinking and creativity in designing EL-appropriate differentiated assessments. Note that products and performances will be differentiated by ELD/P level and, possibly, in terms of content. This differentiation of both language (as indicated by data) and content (as needed) allows the student to enter the learning trajectory that leads to grade-level achievement in both content and language. This two-pronged approach to differentiating assessments (and instruction, addressed in Chapter 6)

Table 5.9 Types of Essential Scaffolds for ELs

Scaffolds for Representation	Scaffolds for Elicitation
• Connections to prior knowledge and experiences (including culture) • Examples of completed work • Authentic items/realia (e.g., an actual plant in a science class) • Photographs and pictures • Models • Graphic organizers (e.g., Venn diagrams, t-charts, concept maps and webs) • Demonstrations • Videos • Simplified reading materials • Manipulatives • Clip art and icons • Simulations and games • Graphs • Charts • Outlines	• Comfortable and safe environment • Meaningful tasks with an authentic purpose • Prompts (e.g., repeat after me, retell the story) • Word banks • Targeted vocabulary and phrases • Sentence starters • Discourse frames (e.g., report format with sentence starters, partially completed outline) • Environmental print for reference • Regular, planned interaction • Thoughtful partnering of students • Heterogeneous grouping • Appropriate acknowledgement of language use and development

provides ELs with access to standards-based achievement, which is their basic civil right (*Lau v. Nichols*, 1974) and is the means by which ELs can engage equitably with content and achieve academically.

In summary, an assessment that is appropriate for ELs merges at least one (modified) content standard with data-driven standards-based language expectations (Figure 5.3).

In order to develop a linguistically differentiated assessment grounded in both content and language standards, teachers must conduct a cross-walk between an individual EL's ELD/P data and the corresponding performance descriptors. By knowing what students are capable of engaging with and producing linguistically, teachers can design meaningful and "do-able" assessments. Table 5.10 provides examples of both products and performances, differentiated by ELD/P level, that can be used across the curriculum to assess ELs' content learning.

These concepts constitute the content of necessary professional development for teachers. Once administrators facilitate this teacher learning, they must ensure their teachers have the freedom to implement their learning in developing and using new tools to obtain accurate information about what ELs know and can do.

Teacher Responsibilities/Actions

Teachers are tasked with determining whether assessments in current use will yield meaningful data about EL learning. When current assessments are deemed inappropriate, these educators must recognize their

Figure 5.3 Development of a Linguistically Differentiated Standards-Based Assessment

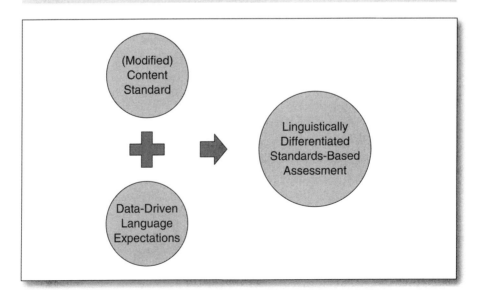

Table 5.10 Linguistically Appropriate Assessments According to TESOL's English Language Development Levels

TESOL English Language Proficiency Levels	PRODUCTS That Demonstrate Achievement of (Modified) Content Standards	PERFORMANCES That Demonstrate Achievement of (Modified) Content Standards
Level 1–Starting: At L1, students initially have limited or no understanding of English. They rarely use English for communication. They respond nonverbally to simple commands, statements, and questions. As their oral comprehension increases, they begin to imitate the verbalizations of others by using single words or simple phrases, and they begin to use English spontaneously. At the earliest stage, these learners construct meaning from text primarily through illustrations, graphs, maps, and tables.	• Draw an illustration • Complete a Venn diagram using pictures • Label a diagram using words or phrases from a word bank	• Point to objects to answer questions • Analyze a process by sequencing pictures • Sort pictures into categories
Level 2–Emerging: At L2, students can understand phrases and short sentences. They can communicate limited information in simple everyday and routine situations by using memorized phrases, groups of words, and formulae. They can use selected simple structures correctly but still systematically produce basic errors. Students begin to use general academic vocabulary and familiar everyday expressions. Errors in writing are present that often hinder communication.	• Complete a pictorially supported concept map using provided phrases and simple sentences • Fill in a pictorially supported outline by analyzing using phrases and simple sentences drawn from environmental print • Write a short poem about a picture using provided key words	• Match clipart pictures and phrases • Categorize pictures labeled with phrases on a t-chart • Describe, using phrases and simple sentences, a self-made poster on a relevant topic using magazine or other pictures
Level 3–Developing: At L3, students understand more complex speech but still may require some repetition. They use English spontaneously but may have difficulty expressing all their thoughts due to a restricted vocabulary and a limited command of language structure. Students at this level speak in simple sentences, which are comprehensible and appropriate, but which are frequently marked by grammatical errors. Proficiency in reading may vary considerably. Students are most successful constructing meaning from texts for which they have background knowledge upon which to build.	• Write an illustrated report • Produce a public service announcement video using visual support • Summarize a piece of linguistically appropriate text, supplemented with a picture or illustration	• Deliver a speech using visual support • Present a self-created model to the class (e.g., a plant cell) • Explain a process using hands-on materials

(Continued)

Table 5.10 (Continued)

TESOL English Language Proficiency Levels	PRODUCTS That Demonstrate Achievement of (Modified) Content Standards	PERFORMANCES That Demonstrate Achievement of (Modified) Content Standards
Level 4–Expanding: At L4, students' language skills are adequate for most day-to-day communication needs. They communicate in English in new or unfamiliar settings but have occasional difficulty with complex structures and abstract academic concepts. Students at this level may read with considerable fluency and are able to locate and identify the specific facts within the text. However, they may not understand texts in which the concepts are presented in a decontextualized manner, the sentence structure is complex, or the vocabulary is abstract or has multiple meanings. They can read independently, but may have occasional comprehension problems, especially when processing grade-level information.	• Compose an essay about an image • Write a descriptive narrative based on an example • Author a letter using a graphic organizer	• Describe a process observed directly • Predict an outcome based on a series of events • Reenact a scene from a book from a different historical perspective
Level 5–Bridging: At L5, students can express themselves fluently and spontaneously on a wide range of personal, general, academic, or social topics in a variety of contexts. They are poised to function in an environment with native speaking peers with minimal language support or guidance. Students have a good command of technical and academic vocabulary as well of idiomatic expressions and colloquialisms. They can produce clear, smoothly flowing, well-structured texts of differing lengths and degrees of linguistic complexity. Errors are minimal, difficult to spot, and generally corrected when they occur.	• Write a research paper • Create a brochure • Compare two points of view on a current event	• Debate a relevant issue • Persuade an audience to adopt a certain point of view • Generalize a scientific principle based on examples

Source: TESOL English Language Proficiency Levels are used with permission.

responsibility to create new tools that allow ELs to demonstrate what they know and can do without full language mastery. Teachers must take full advantage of district-/building-level opportunities to learn the principles of designing EL-appropriate assessments. (The components of these learning opportunities are described above.)

Other Stakeholder Responsibilities/Actions

Other stakeholders are charged with internalizing the shared understanding that many assessments designed for native speakers of English do not provide accurate information about what ELs know and do. Further, they must communicate concerns about the inaccurate assessment of ELs with the wider community, supporting the need for more linguistically accessible assessments. Finally, they have the responsibility to become familiar with and communicate principles of EL-appropriate assessment design, so the wider community can understand shifts in district/school assessment practices.

Stage 8: Developing EL-Appropriate Assessments

Leadership Team Responsibilities/Actions

In order for teachers to put their understanding of appropriate EL assessment into practice, district/school leaders must set and communicate expectations for the district-/school-wide development and use of assessments grounded in content and language standards that have been specifically designed to support ELs in demonstrating what they know and can do at their current ELD/P levels. They are then charged with holding teachers accountable for developing and using these tools.

Teacher Responsibilities/Actions

Having recognized that some assessments may not be linguistically or culturally appropriate for ELs and that there is a need to improve upon past practice, teachers are tasked with creating linguistically differentiated standards-based tools that allow students to fully demonstrate what they know and can do in the content areas. This goal can be met through collaborative efforts organized in the ways that best suit the district/school context.

Other Stakeholder Responsibilities/Actions

As is so often their responsibility, other stakeholders must support the actions taken by administrators and teachers. In Stage 8, this means that these other stakeholders will support the development and implementation of linguistically differentiated content assessments that are grounded in standards and that result in accurate data about what ELs know and can do. In this linguistically accessible way, ELs are afforded access to content standards, resulting in higher levels of EL achievement.

Stage 9: Sharing
EL-Appropriate Assessment Tools

Leadership Team Responsibilities/Actions

In this stage of the process of implementing standards-based assessment and grading of ELs, district/school leaders are urged to acknowledge and reward teachers who design, share, and disseminate differentiated assessment tools that result in accurate data about what ELs know and can do across the curriculum. In so doing, administrators help to ensure that EL academic achievement can increase.

Teacher Responsibilities/Actions

Teachers are encouraged to highlight their success in designing EL-appropriate assessment tools. Further, they can collaboratively share and disseminate these differentiated assessments, developing a repository of assessments to be used district-/school-wide.

Other Stakeholder Responsibilities/Actions

Stakeholders are charged with communicating successes about the development, implementation, and sharing of EL-appropriate assessment tools in the district/school. Further, they must express public appreciation and encouragement to administrators and teachers who support or engage in the design, sharing, and dissemination of differentiated assessment tools that result in more accurate data for ELs.

Stage 10: Establishing Buy-In for
Differentiated Standards-Based Grading

The need for differentiated standards-based grading of ELs is made clear in the following commentary by a secondary educator: "To tell a kid who, for example, starts two grade levels behind and finishes the year one grade level behind, 'Congratulations, you've done two years worth of work in one year, that's outstanding, here's your F.' What's that accomplish?" (Bill Ivey, secondary education, cited in Wormeli, 2006, p. 175). Clearly, data-driven student progress toward meeting standards (in both language and content) must receive positive acknowledgement rather than penalty if the goal is for students to eventually achieve at grade level.

Leadership Team Responsibilities/Actions

District/school leaders must set the tone for the adoption of district/school standards-based grading policies. Only then can these school leaders establish buy-in for the implementation of differentiated standards-based grading. This process may include the following:

- Communicating with teachers, parents, students, and other stakeholders in ways that make sense in their individual contexts
- Providing professional development workshops for teachers
- Facilitating professional learning community book studies
- Bringing in outside experts
- Including aspects of the implementation of standards-based grading in the teacher evaluation process

District/school leaders must then, alongside teachers, parents, and other stakeholders, discuss and develop the district/school rationale for differentiated standards-based grading.

Teacher Responsibilities/Actions

In collaboration with administrators and other stakeholders, teachers must discuss and develop the rationale for differentiated standards-based grading. Then teachers must adhere to the collective rationale for standards-based grading.

Other Stakeholder Responsibilities/Actions

Other stakeholders must discuss and develop, along with administrators and teachers, the district/school rationale for differentiated standards-based grading. They are then tasked with widely communicating and supporting the district/school rationale for standards-based grading. This communication is critically important, as parents and community members have been found to be a barrier to the process of implementing standards-based grading (Peters & Buckmiller, 2014).

Stage 11: Developing Differentiated Standards-Based Grading

Leadership Team Responsibilities/Actions

It is incumbent upon district/school leaders to facilitate and participate in opportunities for teachers to learn about differentiated standards-based grading. In essence, this means that ELs are credited appropriately for meeting (modified) content standards in accordance with their individual ELD/P levels. In other words, these grades may potentially be differentiated in two areas:

1. content standard (when current levels of the student's content knowledge, skills, and abilities and student background factors indicate that modified standards are needed—discussed in Stage 4 above), and

2. ELD/P level (based on the individual student's current ELD/P standards-based data—discussed in Stage 6 above).

Explicitly, this means that if a student completes a (modified) standards-based content assessment (described in Stage 4 above) in accordance with the differentiated linguistic expectations set by the teacher (described in Stage 6 above), that performance warrants full credit (rather than a failing grade because the EL has not met the grade-level content standard designed for native speakers of English). Such achievement positions ELs to continue their incremental advance toward grade-level achievement in both content and English language development.

In order to develop differentiated standards-based grading, teachers must know about

1. standards-based content grading

2. linguistically differentiated grading

The merging of these two types of grading constitutes differentiated standards-based grading.

Standards-Based Grading

A number of researchers provide guidance about the process of standards-based grading (e.g., Guskey & Bailey, 2010; Marzano, 2010; O'Connor, 2009; Wormeli, 2006). These researchers are united in their assertions that grades must represent student achievement based on content standards and that alone. Wormeli (2006) offers "ten approaches to avoid when differentiating assessment and grading" in Chapter 9 of *Fair Isn't Always Equal.* His recommendations include not grading practice (homework); allowing students to redo assignments until mastery is achieved; and leaving nonacademic factors (e.g., behavior, attendance), extra credit, and bonus points out of content grades. In schools/districts where standards-based grading is a new concept, administrators must ensure that they and their educators possess the shared understanding and skill sets needed to implement standards-based grading through professional development opportunities. Specifically, Jung and Guskey's (2010, 2012) work on standards-based grading of exceptional learners, with its emphasis on modified content standards, must be addressed. Only then can educators effectively implement differentiated standards-based grading.

Linguistically Differentiated Grading

In the quest for accurate reporting of EL achievement at the district/school level, teachers must learn how to merge linguistic differentiation with standards-based grading. The process of differentiating the linguistic expectations of assessments based on (modified) content standards was discussed in detail in Stage 6 above and depicted in Figure 5.1. Wormeli essentially calls for such linguistic differentiation when he asserts that teachers should "avoid assessing students in ways that do not accurately indicate their mastery" (2006, p. 121).

Linguistically differentiated standards-based grading involves determining how to credit and report students' achievements on those linguistically differentiated standards-based assessments. The extent to which students meet the content expectations represented by the linguistically differentiated assessment determines the grade for the assessment. The "grade," in this case, refers to a level of accomplishment in meeting the (modified) content standard at the EL's current English language proficiency level (rather than a letter grade). An example is shown in Table 5.11.

Note that these grades indicate performance on assessments that have been linguistically differentiated and possibly differentiated in terms of content expectations. Districts/schools must determine how to

Table 5.11 Example of a Standards-Based Grading Rubric for ELs

(Modified) Standards-Based Performance Level	Description of Content Achievement
Exceeds Standard	EL products and/or performances consistently exceed the (modified) content standard
Consistently Meets Standard	EL products and/or performances consistently meet the (modified) content standard
Progressing Toward Meeting the Standard	EL products and/or performances partially meet the (modified) content standard
Emerging Ability Related to Meeting the Standard	EL products and/or performances minimally meet the (modified) content standard

communicate this differentiation on report cards (e.g., by adding notations about modified linguistic and/or content expectations) and with the wider community.

Teacher Responsibilities/Actions

Teachers must take advantage of the district's/school's opportunities to learn how to develop differentiated standards-based grading, as described above. It is imperative that this process is implemented consistently across the district/school in order to ensure accurate reporting of student learning.

Other Stakeholder Responsibilities/Actions

Based on an understanding of the need for differentiated standards-based grading, other stakeholders must support and widely communicate the development of district/school differentiated standards-based grading.

Stage 12: Implementing Differentiated Standards-Based Grading

Leadership Team Responsibilities

Once the district-/school-wide standards-based grading system has been developed, administrators must lead the implementation by communicating district-/school-wide expectations for differentiated standards-based grading policies and practices with teachers and parents. Leaders must also ensure that their district/school reporting systems are ready for the implementation of differentiated standards-based grading. This might include the addition of additional report card comments that reflect EL and EL parent interests and concerns.

Teacher Responsibilities

Teachers must inform students of standards-based grading policies and practices and then enact the policies/practices adopted by the district/school.

Other Stakeholder Responsibilities

Other stakeholders are charged to stand by district/school administrators and teachers while actively working to support the entire community in understanding the meaning of standards-based grading policies and practices.

Stage 13: Engaging in Ongoing Support for Differentiated Standards-Based Assessment and Grading

Leadership Team Responsibilities/Actions

In order to effectively implement standards-based assessment and grading of ELs, teachers will need ongoing support from district/school leaders. In addition to the continual administrative encouragement that is necessary to effect district-/school-wide change, this support may take the form of additional professional development (e.g., workshops, PLC work), individualized coaching, or assistance with specific challenges on an as-needed basis. Teacher input must be carefully considered and addressed, whatever form the supports take, and administrators must participate actively in all professional development initiatives.

Teacher Responsibilities/Actions

Teachers bear the responsibility of enacting the new district/school initiatives related to differentiated standards-based assessment and grading. Given this responsibility, teachers must take advantage of the supports that administrators put into place to facilitate their work by engaging in those activities, motivated by the will to ensure that ELs' efforts and achievement are appropriately assessed, acknowledged, and reported.

Other Stakeholder Responsibilities/Actions

Other stakeholders must learn what types of refinements are needed as differentiated standards-based assessment and grading take shape in the district/school and communicate this information with the entire community. In this way, other stakeholders can support administrators and teachers in the process of implementing differentiated standards-based assessment and grading with fidelity.

Stage 14: Refining Differentiated Standards-Based Assessment and Grading

Leadership Team Responsibilities/Actions

In the context of an environment that actively supports change, district/school leaders can set district-/school-wide expectations for the ongoing refinement of differentiated standards-based assessment and grading.

Leadership team members are urged to gain input from teachers and other stakeholders about needed refinements. Further, school leaders must note that these refinements will likely occur over time as educators within the district/school become more adept at the use of this approach to assessment and grading. For this reason, leaders are encouraged to stick with the refinement process rather than setting time limits.

Teacher Responsibilities/Actions

Teachers are urged to maintain an open and reflective stance as they implement differentiated standards-based assessment and grading, which will lead to insights that can inform the ongoing refinement process. These insights must be shared with administrators and colleagues to facilitate efforts to refine assessment and grading of ELs.

Other Stakeholder Responsibilities/Actions

Other stakeholders are tasked with supporting the refinement process. This may mean that they take on an advocacy role as they communicate information about the process to the entire community.

Chapter 5 has addressed the alignment of standards-based assessments and grading with ELs' current levels of linguistic and content development. Grounding standards-based instruction in content *and* language development is the focus of Chapter 6.

RESOURCE 5.1 Checklist for Analyzing Language Demands of Assessments

Use this checklist to determine whether your assessment is linguistically appropriate for the ELs who will complete it by asking the following questions informed by the ELD/P performance descriptors used in your district/building. (The goal is to be able to answer "yes" to each statement.)

WORD LEVEL		
1. Is the included vocabulary essential to the standard?	___ yes	___ no
2. Has instruction and use of the word/phrase been explicit and frequent for ELs, with appropriate scaffolding and support (e.g., pictures, models, demonstrations, video clips, peer interaction)?	___ yes	___ no
3. Has the use of the word/phrase been contextualized for ELs (both within instruction and within assessment)?	___ yes	___ no
4. Is there evidence (in written, spoken, or nonverbal form) that the EL(s) who will take the test know(s) the word/phrase?	___ yes	___ no
SENTENCE LEVEL		
5. Is the length of the sentences used in the assessment appropriate to the ELD/P level of the student(s) who will take the test?	___ yes	___ no
6. Are the academic language constructions (e.g., "Contrary to popular belief," "The greater the mass, the greater the force . . .") that are used in the sentences known by the EL(s) who will take the test?	___ yes	___ no
7. Have the tenses used throughout the assessment been mastered by the EL(s) who will take the test (e.g., simple present tense [I go], simple past [I went]); as opposed to overly complicated tenses (e.g., past perfect [I had gone], future perfect [I will have gone])?	___ yes	___ no
8. Is the complexity of the sentences used in the assessment appropriate for the EL(s) who will take the test?	___ yes	___ no
DISCOURSE (EXTENDED EXPRESSION) LEVEL		
9. Is the organization of the discourse (e.g., paragraph, essay, lab report) accessible to the ELs who will complete the assessment?	___ yes	___ no
10. Is the length of the discourse aligned with the linguistic stamina of the EL(s) who will complete the assessment?	___ yes	___ no
11. Is the variety of sentence types comprehensible to and appropriate for the EL(s) who will complete the assessment?	___ yes	___ no
12. Is the language used to connect and transition between ideas in the text comprehensible to the EL(s) who will complete the assessment?	___ yes	___ no
13. Has the discourse-level language of the assessment been explicitly taught to ELs in meaningful ways?	___ yes	___ no
14. Have students been held accountable in class for using the discourse-level language of the assessment?	___ yes	___ no

RESOURCE 5.2 Template for Determining a Student's Content Instructional Level

Student Name: _____			
Current level of knowledge, skills, and abilities in the content area and implications for learning	*Key background characteristics and implications for learning*	*Extent to which the student is prepared to meet the content standard*	*Next logical step: A modified content standard* (refer to learning progressions or other relevant resources for guidance)

Ground Standards-Based Instruction in Content *and* Language Development

6

Teachers must first be mindful of the fundamental challenge that ELs who receive all-English instruction face as they attempt to learn academic content while becoming increasingly proficient in English. The goal should be to make academic content as accessible as possible for those students and promote oral and written English language development as students learn academic content.

(Coleman & Goldenberg, 2012, p. 48)

In order to afford English learners access to the core content curricula, as is their basic civil right, EL-data-driven instruction must be delivered in accessible ways. This means that while focusing on district-wide content standards, attention must be paid to adjusting the linguistic demands of that instruction based on students' current linguistic developmental levels *and* adjusting the content demands of those standards to align with ELs' current content knowledge, skills, and abilities.

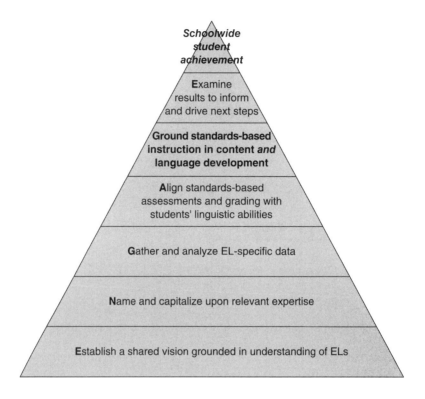

In addition to describing key processes associated with assessment and grading, Chapter 5 discussed five key action steps that serve as a foundation for linguistically differentiated standards-based instruction:

- Setting high expectations
- Implementing collaboration
- Developing or enhancing knowledge of content standards
- Modifying content standards, as needed
- Developing knowledge of linguistic differentiation

This chapter provides guidance about stages specific to the grounding of standards-based instruction in content *and* language development. Specific responsibilities for leadership teams, teachers, and other stakeholders are discussed. Table 6.1 lists these stages and associated responsibilities.

STAGE 1: ENSURING THAT CURRICULAR DESIGN ALIGNS WITH BEST PRACTICES FOR ELS

For ELLs in particular, the academic language competencies embodied in the standards require systemic, district-wide approaches to curriculum design and instructional delivery that intertwine language development and content. . . . This potential will only be realized if policy leaders and practitioners carefully examine programs and practices and evaluate their impact on ELLs' progress in meeting the standards.

(Haynes, 2012, p. 2)

Haynes makes clear the need for administrators, teachers, and other stakeholders to collaboratively analyze district-/school-wide systems for their efficacy in providing ELs with simultaneous opportunities to

Table 6.1 Stages and Areas of Responsibility *and* Action for Grounding Standards-Based Instruction in Content and Language Development

Stages / Areas of Responsibility	Leadership Team Responsibilities	Teacher Responsibilities	Other Stakeholder Responsibilities (e.g., school board members, parents)
1. Ensuring that curricular design aligns with best practices for ELs	Call for and facilitate curricular design that aligns with best practices for ELs; lead the process of necessary curricular revision/redesign	Contribute to necessary curricular revision/redesign that aligns with best practices for ELs	Learn about EL best practices in curricular design; contribute to the revision/redesign process where appropriate; communicate information about the process to the wider community
2. Gathering EL-appropriate resources for (modified) standards-based instruction	Support and facilitate the gathering of EL-appropriate resources for (modified) standards-based instruction	Contribute to the gathering of EL-appropriate resources for (modified) standards-based instruction	Support and facilitate the gathering of EL-appropriate resources for (modified) standards-based instruction
3. Building expertise in linguistically differentiated teaching strategies and lesson planning for (modified) standards-based instruction	Provide and attend needed professional development on linguistically differentiated (modified) standards-based teaching strategies and lesson planning	Actively participate in professional development on linguistically differentiated (modified) standards-based teaching strategies and lesson planning, building the ability to use the strategies effectively	Learn about linguistically differentiated (modified) standards-based teaching strategies and lesson planning; communicate their value to the wider community

(Continued)

Table 6.1 (Continued)

Stages / Areas of Responsibility	Leadership Team Responsibilities	Teacher Responsibilities	Other Stakeholder Responsibilities (e.g., school board members, parents)
4. Implementing linguistically differentiated (modified) standards-based instruction (in addition to language instruction educational programs)	Set and communicate district-/school-wide expectations for linguistically differentiated (modified) standards-based instruction; guide and support teachers in enacting this type of instruction	Implement linguistically differentiated (modified) standards-based instruction	Support linguistically differentiated (modified) standards-based instruction through communication and advocacy in the wider community
5. Engaging in ongoing support for linguistically differentiated (modified) standards-based instruction	Based on monitoring data, support teachers in meeting their responsibilities to enact linguistically differentiated (modified) standards-based teaching through ongoing professional development; participate in these learning opportunities	Assist administrators in prioritizing and designing ongoing professional development; actively participate in professional development opportunities to enhance linguistically differentiated (modified) standards-based instruction	Gain understanding of the enhancements needed for effective linguistically differentiated (modified) standards-based instruction; support efforts to facilitate those enhancements
6. Refining linguistically differentiated (modified) standards-based instruction	Set and communicate expectations district-/school-wide for the continual refinement of linguistically differentiated (modified) standards-based instruction	Refine implementation of linguistically differentiated (modified) standards-based instruction	Support refinements to linguistically differentiated (modified) standards-based instruction; communicate them to the entire community

develop their knowledge of both the English language and standards-based content. Any part of the district's/school's instruction and assessment system that is found wanting must be redesigned if the goal of EL academic achievement is to be met. The point of entry for this analysis must be the curriculum, as it serves as the foundation for instruction and assessment.

Leadership Team Responsibilities

District/school leaders must initiate and guide this curricular analysis. It is their responsibility to ensure that all curricula align with EL best practices. Haynes (2012) asserts that

> significant improvements in ELLs' language and content-area learning require a major shift to coursework that promotes discourse-rich, experiential learning, in which the learner has opportunities to interact and reflect on information and ideas through observation and inquiry. (p. 7)

Leaders are urged to use these or other EL-specific criteria as they lead the analysis of current district/school curricula. Based on the findings of this work, changes can be implemented to ensure that curriculum is designed to support the academic achievement of ELs. (A simple template for use in this essential curricular analysis and planning for needed revision/redesign is provided in Resource 6.1.) Leadership team members must then direct or delegate the process of necessary curricular revision/redesign.

Teacher Responsibilities

Teachers must contribute to curricular revision/redesign that aligns with best practice for ELs. This will require input from teachers with a wide variety of expertise.

Other Stakeholder Responsibilities

Other stakeholders bear several responsibilities related to curricular design. These include the need to learn about EL best practices in curricular design, contribute to the revision/redesign process where appropriate, and communicate information about the process to the wider community.

STAGE 2: GATHERING EL-APPROPRIATE RESOURCES FOR (MODIFIED) STANDARDS-BASED INSTRUCTION

Leadership Team Responsibilities

Adequate materials have been found to be a key characteristic of schools that successfully support the learning of ELs (EdSource, 2007). District/school leaders must ensure that these essential teaching resources are available to support EL access to standards-based learning, whether the standards are modified or at grade level. In order to accomplish this goal, leaders may need to request specific allocations for the purchase of appropriate materials, find outside funding sources, or brainstorm other means of obtaining these essential instructional resources.

Gordon and Morales (2012) list several fundamental considerations for choosing materials for ELs: student age, student English language development/proficiency (ELD/P level), native language background and use in current schooling, and standards-based curricular demands. Materials must be age appropriate and tied to appropriate curricular standards. The level of students' ELD/P drives the selection of materials that will be accessible; materials should be matched to students' capabilities in English. Sets of books that focus on the same topic but are at different reading levels have great utility for teachers who serve ELs at differing ELD/P levels. If students can read in their native languages, materials in those languages can sometimes help students to grasp standards-based content. Such materials must be provided in bilingual settings. Potential sources of this range of resources are listed in Appendix 6.1.

Teacher Responsibilities

Teachers can and should play a significant role in gathering the resources needed for linguistically differentiated (modified) standards-based instruction. Their insights about the exact kinds of materials that will best support EL learning represent a rich resource in this stage of grounding instruction to ELs' current levels of content and language development.

Other Stakeholder Responsibilities

Like administrators, other stakeholders are charged with supporting and facilitating the acquisition of EL-appropriate instructional resources. In addition to awareness about useful materials, they may well have personal and/or professional connections to individuals and organizations that can be drawn upon to secure needed resources.

STAGE 3: BUILDING EXPERTISE IN LINGUISTICALLY DIFFERENTIATED TEACHING STRATEGIES AND LESSON PLANNING FOR (MODIFIED) STANDARDS-BASED INSTRUCTION

Leadership Team Responsibilities

Referencing reviews of research, Calderón, Slavin, and Sánchez (2011) assert that, for teachers of ELs, the most beneficial professional development includes the following (p. 114):

- Opportunities for hands-on practice with teaching techniques readily applicable in their classrooms
- In-class demonstrations with their own or a colleague's students
- Personalized coaching

District/school leaders are urged to keep this in mind when determining how to facilitate teacher knowledge and skill in utilizing differentiated teaching strategies.

A key mechanism for planning and implementing linguistic differentiation is the use of the *language objective.* Language objectives assist teachers and students in purposefully developing the language skills necessary for participation in and demonstration of content learning. Kinsella and Singer (2011) clarify that a language objective consists of both a function and a language target. Put another way,

language objective	=	what students will do with language	+	the kinds of language they will use to do it

To determine what language objectives a given lesson calls for, teachers can consider the language that ELs will need both for learning activities and for demonstrating that they have learned content.

These language objectives are differentiated according to ELD/P level. They are designed to facilitate success on the differentiated expectations during and after the lesson and to support *all* students in the class (not only ELs) in their work to develop increasingly sophisticated academic language.

Recall Chandra, the third-grade Bhutanese student described in Chapter 2. Her English language development levels are as follows:

- Listening = 3
- Speaking = 3
- Reading = 2
- Writing = 1

For a lesson focused on shapes, their names, their characteristics, and their similarities and differences, a sample content objective could be this:

- Explain how a square and a rhombus are similar and different.

In order for Chandra to demonstrate that she has mastered this objective, the following language objectives (differentiated for a Level 3 speaker) could be incorporated into the lesson:

- Describe the sides of a square and a rhombus using a simple sentence.
- Describe the angles of a square and a rhombus using a simple sentence.

- State what is the same about these two shapes using a simple sentence.
- State what can be different about these two shapes using a simple sentence.

Note that the language objectives include language functions (*describe, state*) *and* target language (*using a simple sentence*).

By clearly explicating and teaching these differentiated language objectives, teachers empower ELs to demonstrate what they know and can do in the content areas. The next question is, "How do I go about teaching this sort of differentiated standards-based lesson?"

One way that teaching can be linguistically differentiated for ELs is through collaboration and coteaching. Honigsfeld and Dove (2010) offer specific guidance for the implementation of a variety of models of collaboration and coteaching designed to support the academic achievement of ELs. These approaches could take center stage in professional development focused on differentiated instruction.

In addition to working collaboratively, teachers can implement a variety of teaching strategies independently. Informed by the TESOL performance descriptors for English language proficiency at Levels 1–5, Table 6.2 lists a set of powerful strategies designed to facilitate EL access to standards-based learning academic achievement. Based on research that supports the use of both direct instruction and interaction to teach reading and writing to ELs (Genessee & Riches, 2006), these instructional strategies are grouped into two categories:

1. Strategies that support the *representation* of (modified) content standards (tied to representation)

2. Strategies that support the *elicitation* of responses and language related to (modified) content standards (tied to interaction)

Note that strategies listed for ELs at lower ELD/P levels can also be used to support the learning of ELs at higher levels, when appropriate.

Table 6.2 Instructional Strategies for Linguistic Differentiation

TESOL English Language Development/Proficiency (ELD/P) Levels	Strategies to Support *Representation* of (Modified) Content Standards	Strategies to Support *Elicitation* of Responses and Language Related to (Modified) Content Standards
For ELs at All Levels	• Connections to prior knowledge/experiences (including culture) • Authentic items/realia (real objects) • Photographs/pictures • Clipart/icons • Videos with clear connections between language and visuals • Models/modeling • Demonstrations • Manipulatives • Hands-on activities • Explicit feedback on learning (at the student's instructional level)	• Safe, welcoming environment • Meaningful tasks with an authentic purpose • Pictorially supported environmental print • Regular, planned interaction • Thoughtful partnering of students • Heterogeneous grouping • Clear speech that is not overly fast • Appropriate acknowledgement of language use and development • Instructional conversations
Level 1—Starting: At L1, students initially have limited or no understanding of English. They rarely use English for communication. They respond nonverbally to simple commands, statements, and questions. As their oral comprehension increases, they begin to imitate the verbalizations of others by using single words or simple phrases, and they begin to use English spontaneously. At the earliest stage, these learners construct meaning from text primarily through illustrations, graphs, maps, and tables.	• Picture and word cards (for teaching vocabulary) • T-chart or Venn diagram with pictures (students can label with words or phrases) • Examples of completed assignments differentiated for Level 1	• Pictures with modeling (e.g., *Point to the living/nonliving thing* [as teacher points]) • "Repeat after me" with objects, photos, et cetera • Yes–no questions with visual support (e.g., *Is this a laptop?*)
Level 2—Emerging: At L2, students can understand phrases and short sentences. They can communicate limited information in simple everyday and routine situations by using memorized	• Print materials that include pictures labeled with pretaught language (words, phrases, short sentences)	• Sentence starters for oral or written production (focus on phrases or short sentences, such as *First, I ___. Second, I ___.*)

(Continued)

Table 6.2 (Continued)

TESOL English Language Development/Proficiency (ELD/P) Levels	Strategies to Support *Representation* of (Modified) Content Standards	Strategies to Support *Elicitation* of Responses and Language Related to (Modified) Content Standards
phrases, groups of words, and formulae. They can use selected simple structures correctly but still systematically produce basic errors. Students begin to use general academic vocabulary and familiar everyday expressions. Errors in writing are present that often hinder communication.	• Pictorially supported concept maps that students can label with provided, pretaught phrases or simple sentences • Examples of completed assignments differentiated for Level 2	• Simple, visually supported questions that call for answers in the form of phrases or simple sentences (e.g., *What is this called?* [holding up a piece of lab equipment]) • Routine interaction opportunities (e.g., think–pair–share) supported by environmental print (e.g., class-developed poster with phrases needed to participate)
Level 3—Developing: At L3, students understand more complex speech but still may require some repetition. They use English spontaneously but may have difficulty expressing all their thoughts due to a restricted vocabulary and a limited command of language structure. Students at this level speak in simple sentences, which are comprehensible and appropriate, but which are frequently marked by grammatical errors. Proficiency in reading may vary considerably. Students are most successful constructing meaning from texts for which they have background knowledge upon which to build.	• Print materials that include pictures that match simple text • Recycling of new vocabulary in the lesson, with consistent teacher reference to the pictorially supported word wall • Examples of completed assignments differentiated for Level 3	• Sentence starters for oral or written production (focus on simple sentences, such as *The first step is ___.*) • Paragraph frames to support written production (focus on the completion of simple sentences with pretaught, visually supported content vocabulary) • Pictures about familiar topics (including pretaught academic content) about which students can talk or write using well-learned vocabulary/language and pictorially supported environmental print
Level 4—Expanding: At L4, students' language skills are adequate for most day-to-day communication needs. They communicate in English in new or unfamiliar settings but have occasional difficulty with complex	• Print materials that make use of simple, compound, and some complex sentence structures and include visual support for abstract concepts, in	• Questions that include key language for students to use in the answer and that are supported visually (e.g., *What can you tell me about the process of photosynthesis?*)

TESOL English Language Development/Proficiency (ELD/P) Levels	Strategies to Support *Representation* of (Modified) Content Standards	Strategies to Support *Elicitation* of Responses and Language Related to (Modified) Content Standards
structures and abstract academic concepts. Students at this level may read with considerable fluency and are able to locate and identify the specific facts within the text. However, they may not understand texts in which the concepts are presented in a decontextualized manner, the sentence structure is complex, or the vocabulary is abstract or has multiple meanings. They can read independently but may have occasional comprehension problems, especially when processing grade-level information.	particular (materials may need to be below grade level) • Partially completed outlines with a pictorially supported language bank (for taking notes in minilectures or while reading content materials) • Examples of completed assignments differentiated for Level 4	• Discourse frames (for extended expression, such as lab reports, a five-paragraph essay) that provide students with key language (e.g., essential content vocabulary, transition words) • Explicit contextualized instruction about idiomatic language and colloquialisms to support advances toward full English language proficiency
Level 5—Bridging: At L5, students can express themselves fluently and spontaneously on a wide range of personal, general, academic, or social topics in a variety of contexts. They are poised to function in an environment with native speaking peers with minimal language support or guidance. Students have a good command of technical and academic vocabulary as well of idiomatic expressions and colloquialisms. They can produce clear, smoothly flowing, well-structured texts of differing lengths and degrees of linguistic complexity. Errors are minimal, difficult to spot, and generally corrected when they occur.	• Grade-level materials that include visual support for very new or abstract concepts • Targeting of idiosyncratic linguistic needs (e.g., using Latin roots to assist students in learning scientific content vocabulary) • Examples of completed assignments differentiated for Level 5	• Grade-level questions supported by environmental print and visuals • Assignment sheets that call for grade-level language production but clarify differentiated scoring • Holding students accountable to produce language orally and in writing that maximizes their Level 5 capability (e.g., produce extended discourse, include targeted vocabulary, generate a range of sentence types) • Refusal to accept one-word answers

Source: TESOL ELD/P levels are used with permission.

District/school leaders can facilitate learning of any and all of these strategies by integrating demonstrations, application, and coaching with professional development workshops, professional learning communities, book studies, et cetera. They are urged to participate in these opportunities as well, in order to facilitate their work as instructional leaders.

For readers interested in additional EL teaching strategies, Fairbairn and Jones-Vo (2010) provide extensive guidance with a poster of strategies for both instruction and assessment for each ELD/P level. Many other resources that present EL teaching strategies are also available. A list of teacher resources focused on EL teaching strategies is provided in Appendix 6.2 at the end of the chapter.

In addition to specific teaching strategies, EL-responsive research-based practices must be incorporated into lesson planning. The literature reveals several key teaching practices that support the success of ELs:

1. The ongoing use of data to inform instruction (Calderón et al., 2011; EdSource, 2007)

2. The development of oral language and vocabulary (Calderón et al., 2011; Goldenberg, 2008)

3. The incorporation of cooperative learning (Calderón et al., 2011; Rothstein-Fisch & Trumbull, 2008)

4. The provision of supplementary instruction to students who need it (Calderón et al., 2011)

The research literature clarifies that the ongoing use of data to inform instruction is a hallmark of schools that support EL success. Chapter 4 outlined this process in detail, and administrators must support these practices on a continual basis.

Teachers must continually strive to build ELs' oral language skills and vocabulary. This work is supported by the work of leadership teams that facilitate professional development focused on the implementation of the differentiated strategies listed in Table 6.2.

Cooperative learning is a technique that facilitates EL learning on multiple levels; it is culturally responsive for many ELs and facilitates interaction as students coconstruct understanding of new concepts. The differentiated strategies listed above align with and support the use of cooperative learning.

ELs at beginning ELD/P levels who are learning language and content through linguistically differentiated instruction focused on *modified* content standards likely require supplementary learning opportunities if they are to achieve academically. This is their basic civil right (*Lau v. Nichols*, 1974). In today's districts/schools, this supplementary instruction may be part of the implementation of multitiered systems of support (MTSS), also referred to as response to intervention (RTI). (For more information, see one of the many books on the subject, such as Bender & Shore, 2007, or Mellard & Johnson, 2008.)

The overarching principle for RTI for ELs is *flexibility* (Nguyen, 2013). That is, teachers must meet the needs of ELs at their individual developmental levels as indicated by performance, implementing EL-specific strategies in the mainstream classroom. It is essential that teachers, administrators, and other stakeholders recognize that Tier 1 (universal instruction) within the RTI model includes English language instruction *and* differentiated content instruction. That is, English development support and differentiated standards-based content instruction are not to be considered extras or bonuses for ELs only if time allows; they are part of the general education that must be provided to these students as part of their core instruction (Nguyen, 2013).

When ELs are provided with language education instructional programming and linguistically differentiated content instruction appropriate to their needs and continue to need additional support, Tier 2 interventions are warranted. However, these interventions must be EL-specific. That is, predesigned interventions or protocols created for native speakers of English must be carefully interrogated using the EL Lens before they are applied to ELs. (For example, intensive decontextualized phonics drill is typically inappropriate for ELs, who require contextualized instruction to maximize their learning.)

To reiterate, planning for linguistically differentiated instruction focused on (modified) content standards should be driven by recent and relevant data, include a focus on the development of oral language and vocabulary, make use of cooperative learning, and provide supplementary instruction for those who need it. These practices can and should be included in lesson plan templates used by teachers.

Teacher Responsibilities

Teachers must actively participate in professional development opportunities that focus on building their toolkits of teaching strategies and lesson planning for linguistically differentiating instruction based on (modified) standards. This will require discussion and reflection about how, when, and why to use each strategy within lesson plans, as well as direct work with different strategies in the context of EL-responsive lesson plans.

Other Stakeholder Responsibilities

Other stakeholders are tasked with learning about strategies and lesson planning for linguistically differentiated instruction focused on (modified) standards. This will empower them to communicate the value of these practices to the wider community.

STAGE 4: IMPLEMENTING LINGUISTICALLY DIFFERENTIATED (MODIFIED) STANDARDS-BASED INSTRUCTION

Districts serving ELs must have language instruction education programs (LIEPs) in place. There are many models for these programs, and guidance for developing LIEPs is given in detail elsewhere (e.g., Collier & Thomas, 2009; Custodio, 2011). The aim of this section is to discuss the implementation of linguistically differentiated instruction grounded in (modified) content standards.

Leadership Team Responsibilities

District/school leadership team members are responsible for setting and communicating district-/school-wide expectations for linguistically differentiated standards-based instruction that incorporates the four research-based practices listed in the previous section. During this implementation, these individuals must truly embody the role of instructional leader, offering guidance and support to teachers as they work to implement new instructional approaches in a step-by-step manner (rather than trying to change everything at once). A checklist such as that in Resource 6.2 at the end of the chapter can be used by both administrators and teachers in this implementation stage.

Teacher Responsibilities

Teachers must break down difficult tasks into manageable segments, facilitate productive discussions, provide meaningful and appropriate feedback, and explicitly model and support student production of language. They should provide instructional support to students in close reading of complex text by using extensive pre-reading activities and conversations to leverage English learners' existing background knowledge. In addition, students gain access to the concepts, vocabulary, and ideas encoded in complex text through multiple opportunities during and after reading to engage in sense making with their classmates and teachers.

(Haynes, 2012, pp. 9–10)

Haynes outlines the complexities of effectively teaching ELs. This multifaceted work requires teachers to "think on their feet" in order to meet the needs of ELs with different backgrounds and different levels of language and content development. Teachers are urged to use their learning of research-based practices and linguistic differentiated teaching strategies in step-by-step fashion, allowing themselves the time to gradually increase the range of strategies employed. This will allow them to focus their efforts on specific aspects of each lesson, rather than feeling overwhelmed by the unrealistic notion of having to change everything at once. Administrators are charged with guiding and supporting this measured application of new learning in the classroom.

Other Stakeholder Responsibilities

Other stakeholders play a key role in supporting the implementation of new practices district-/school-wide. They must not only communicate the implementation process to the wider community, but also advocate for these essential changes in practice.

STAGE 5: ENGAGING IN ONGOING SUPPORT FOR LINGUISTICALLY DIFFERENTIATED (MODIFIED) STANDARDS-BASED INSTRUCTION

Leadership Team Responsibilities

As the implementation process proceeds, the insights that district/ school leaders glean through their instructional leadership (e.g., using the checklist in Resource 6.2 to guide and support the implementation process) will reveal specific needs for ongoing professional development. Leaders are urged to ensure that this ongoing professional development does not present new and different information, but instead deepens understanding of the linguistic differentiation strategies and research-based practices discussed in Stage 3 above. The form that this ongoing support takes will depend upon the specific needs and the context. Wise leaders will seek explicit teacher input in determining how to best provide this professional development. They will then participate in these initiatives themselves, in order to enhance their work as instructional leaders.

Teacher Responsibilities

By reflecting on their practice and communicating with one another, teachers can assist administrators in prioritizing and designing professional development to support the ongoing implementation process. Through their active engagement in these activities, teachers can enhance their understanding of linguistically differentiated standards-based instruction.

Other Stakeholder Responsibilities

The task of other stakeholders in Stage 5 is to gain understanding of the enhancements needed for effective linguistically differentiated standards-based instruction. Against this backdrop, these individuals can support efforts to facilitate those refinements, resulting in EL access to standards-based instruction and, ultimately, increased student achievement.

STAGE 6: REFINING LINGUISTICALLY DIFFERENTIATED (MODIFIED) STANDARDS-BASED INSTRUCTION

Leadership Team Responsibilities

Having provided multiple layers of support for teacher implementation of linguistically differentiated standards-based instruction, district/school leaders are poised to set and communicate district-/school-wide expectations for the continual refinement of this new practice. Accountability for progress toward common goals has been deemed to be an element of effective practice for ELs (Calderón et al., 2011, p. 110).

Teacher Responsibilities

In the context of a supportive environment and under the guidance of a true instructional leader, teachers can continue to refine their linguistically differentiated standards-based instruction. Having been provided with multiple supports, teachers are able to take steps to better engage ELs in learning both language and content.

Other Stakeholder Responsibilities

Other stakeholders are charged with supporting the refinements to this new teaching approach. By communicating these enhancements to the teaching/learning process, these individuals can strengthen current momentum to fuel the enactment of this change.

The six stages described in this chapter mark the end of the initial cycle of new practices represented by the ENGAGE model. The next, final chapter will address the analysis of the process thus far in order to inform and drive next steps.

RESOURCE 6.1 Template for Curricular Analysis

This template, based on the EL curricular recommendations of Haynes (2012), can be used to determine the extent to which curricula are appropriate for ELs and to plan next steps in the curriculum revision/redesign process.

Curricular Characteristic	Extent to Which the Characteristic Is Present	Next Steps
Discourse-rich	☐ consistently ☐ often ☐ sometimes ☐ rarely ☐ never	
Experiential	☐ consistently ☐ often ☐ sometimes ☐ rarely ☐ never	
Includes opportunities for interaction	☐ consistently ☐ often ☐ sometimes ☐ rarely ☐ never	
Includes opportunities for reflection	☐ consistently ☐ often ☐ sometimes ☐ rarely ☐ never	
Requires observation	☐ consistently ☐ often ☐ sometimes ☐ rarely ☐ never	
Requires inquiry	☐ consistently ☐ often ☐ sometimes ☐ rarely ☐ never	

RESOURCE 6.2 Checklist for Implementing Research-Based Practices and Linguistically Differentiated Teaching Strategies in Standards-Based Lesson Plans

Strategies	Strategies to Support Representation of (Modified) Content Standards	Strategies to Support Elicitation of Responses and Language Related to (Modified) Content Standards
Practices		
Ongoing use of data to inform instruction	□ consistently □ often □ sometimes □ rarely □ never Notes:	□ consistently □ often □ sometimes □ rarely □ never Notes:
Development of oral language and vocabulary	□ consistently □ often □ sometimes □ rarely □ never Notes:	□ consistently □ often □ sometimes □ rarely □ never Notes:
Incorporation of cooperative learning	□ consistently □ often □ sometimes □ rarely □ never Notes:	□ consistently □ often □ sometimes □ rarely □ never Notes:
Provision of supplementary instruction to students who need it	□ consistently □ often □ sometimes □ rarely □ never Notes:	□ consistently □ often □ sometimes □ rarely □ never Notes:

APPENDIX 6.1 Sources of EL-Appropriate Resources

Print Materials

Asia for Kids (a variety of books, materials, and gifts representing a range of Asian languages and cultures)
4480 Lake Forest Dr. #302
Cincinnati, OH 45242
203–821–3473
www.asiaforkids.com

Hampton-Brown Edge (reading/language arts for students reading below grade level, materials available in Spanish; registration required)
(Part of National Geographic Learning)
10650 Toebben Drive
Independence, KY 41051
888–915–3276
www.ngsptechnology.com

Millmark Education (ConceptLinks—science books and materials aligned with TESOL standards)
7101 Wisconsin Avenue, Suite 1204
Bethesda, MD 20814
1–877–322–8020
www.millmarkeducation.com

Multi-cultural Books and Videos (materials available in a variety of languages, bilingual books)
30007 John R Road
Madison Heights, MI 48071
800–567–2220
www.multiculturalbooksandvideos.com/mcbv/home/option1/home

National Geographic Learning (a variety of materials suitable for ELs—see specific URLs below)
10650 Toebben Drive
Independence, KY 41051
888–915–3276
http://ngl.cengage.com/search/showresults.do?N=200+4294918395 (books at a variety of reading levels on various topics, ESL language and grammar teaching materials)
www.ngsptechnology.com/tabid/1261/default.aspx (materials for ELs who are newcomers to the United States)

Okapi Educational Publishing (a range of materials to support literacy development)
42381 Rio Nedo
Temecula, CA 92590
866–652–7436
www.myokapi.com

(Continued)

APPENDIX 6.1 (Continued)

Perfection Learning (a variety of materials—see URLs below)

1000 North Second Avenue

Logan, IA 51546

800–831–4190

www.perfectionlearning.com/ell-reading-corner (collection of beginning books with teacher handbook)

www.perfectionlearning.com/high-interest-low-reading%20Level (high-interest, low reading-level books)

www.perfectionlearning.com/browse.php?categoryID=3915&level=2&parent=2622 (graphic fiction and nonfiction)

Rigby (Houghton Mifflin Harcourt) (On Our Way to English—full program for teaching ESL, built on Common Core State Standards)

Specialized Curriculum Group

9205 Southpark Center Loop

Orlando, FL 32819

800–289–4490

www.hmhco.com/shop/education-curriculum/english-language-learners/on-our-way-to-english

Saddleback Educational Publishing (high-interest, low reading-level books)

3120-A Pullman Street

Costa Mesa, CA 92626

888–734–4010

www.sdlback.com/hi-lo-reading

Santillana USA Publishing (books in Spanish)

2023 NW 84th Avenue

Doral, FL 33122

800–245–8584

www.santillanausa.com

Online Resources

Colorin Colorado—a range of Spanish–English bilingual resources for teachers and families

www.colorincolorado.org

International Children's Digital Library—digital books in many languages, bilingual books

http://en.childrenslibrary.org

Pebble Go—nonfiction read-aloud books with associated videos and other instructional materials to support student research (four databases: animals, earth and space, biographies, social studies)

www.pebblego.com

(Subscription required, but free trial available)

NetTrekker—reviewed websites suitable for K–12 students, search capability for Spanish websites

school.nettrekker.com

(Subscription required)

TruFlix—read-aloud books on a variety of topics
tfx.grolier.com

(Subscription required, but free trial available)

Mackin VIA—Starwalk and Tales 2 Go databases include read-aloud books in English and Spanish as well as Spanish–English bilingual books

www.mackinvia.com

(Subscription required)

APPENDIX 6.2 Example Resources Focused on EL Teaching Strategies

Diaz-Rico, L. T. (2013). *Strategies for teaching English learners* (3rd ed.). Boston, MA: Pearson.

Dove, M. G., & Honigsfeld, A. (2013). *Common core for the not-so-common learner, Grades K–5*. Thousand Oaks, CA: Corwin.

Fairbairn, S., & Jones-Vo, S. (2010). *Differentiating instruction and assessment for English language learners: A guide for K–12 teachers*. Philadelphia, PA: Caslon.

Gregory, G. H., & Burkman, A. (2012). *Differentiated literacy strategies for English language learners, Grades K–6*. Thousand Oaks, CA: Corwin.

Gregory, G. H., & Burkman, A. (2012). *Differentiated literacy strategies for English language learners, Grades 7–12*. Thousand Oaks, CA: Corwin.

Herrell, A. L., & Jordan, M. (2012). *50 strategies for teaching English language learners* (4th ed.). Boston, MA: Pearson.

Kottler, E., Kottler, J. A., & Street, C. (2008). *English language learners in your classroom: Strategies that work* (3rd ed.). Thousand Oaks, CA: Corwin.

Reiss. J. (2012). *Content strategies for English language learners: Teaching for academic success in secondary school* (2nd ed.). Boston, MA: Pearson.

Reyes, S. A., & Vallone, T. L. (2008). *Constructivist strategies for teaching English learners*. Thousand Oaks, CA: Corwin.

Wagner, S., & King, T. (2012). *Implementing effective instruction for English language learners: 12 key practices for administrators, teachers, and leadership teams*. Philadelphia, PA: Caslon.

Examine Results to Inform and Drive Next Steps   7

It is revealing how accountability plays itself out. It turns out that blatant accountability focusing on tests, standards and the like is not the best way to get results. Rather, successful systems combine strategies of capacity building and transparency of results and practice. . . . There is no greater motivator than internal accountability to oneself and one's peers. It makes for a better profession, and it makes for a better system.

(Fullan, 2011b, p. 8)

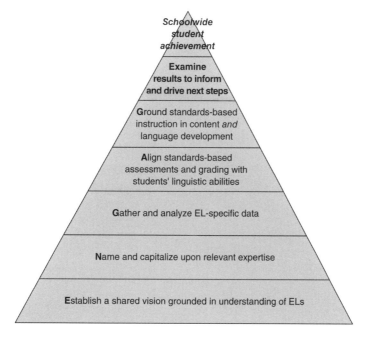

Schoolwide
student
achievement

**Examine
results to inform
and drive next steps**

Ground standards-based
instruction in content *and*
language development

Align standards-based
assessments and grading with
students' linguistic abilities

Gather and analyze EL-specific data

Name and capitalize upon relevant expertise

Establish a shared vision grounded in understanding of ELs

Research supports the examination of results in this last step of the ENGAGE model by confirming that monitoring implementation and outcomes is an element of effective practice for ELs (Calderón, Slavin, & Sánchez, 2011, p. 116). Leadership teams, teachers, and other stakeholders each contribute to this step by providing input in meetings and through other means (e.g., email) and by completing surveys developed at the district/school level. Any step in the model may warrant refinement based on insights gained throughout the process of implementation and from data collected as part of this examination process.

To begin this examination, leaders, teachers, and other stakeholders must analyze each step in the ENGAGE model, first focusing on the ultimate goal of the ENGAGE model: increased district-/school-wide student achievement. The model's focus on this goal remains consistent throughout each part of the model's implementation (see the opening figure).

The examination of results and determination of next steps can be undertaken in whatever way best fits the district/school context. However, it is recommended that administrators, teachers, and other stakeholders organize this process around key questions tied to each part of the ENGAGE model, beginning with a look at the ultimate goal of the model. Table 7.1 shows a list of questions that can serve as a springboard for analysis, discussion, and planning. Districts/schools are encouraged to use this guidance as a starting point for their work, adding to it where appropriate. (A template for this process is provided in Resource 7.1 at the end of the chapter.)

The process of examining data, determining next steps, and carrying these steps out does not have a specific time limit. This process may be conducted on an ongoing basis as each step in the model is addressed or may be undertaken after the first five steps in the model have been addressed. Readers are reminded that the implementation of the model is meant to take whatever form best suits the specific context of the district/school that has undertaken the change process.

Insights gleaned from the examination of results must then be incorporated into ongoing practice in order to make improvements that will positively impact EL academic achievement. This examination process can then be undertaken in a cyclical fashion over time, in order to continually adjust to current realities.

By implementing the ENGAGE model, administrators, teachers, and other stakeholders are able to provide ELs with access to standards-based learning, addressing their civil rights and ensuring that they have the opportunity to reach their full potential.

Table 7.1 Key Questions to Guide Examination of Results to Inform Next Steps

Goal/Step in the ENGAGE Model	Guiding Questions	Potential Data Sources

Ultimate Goal: Increased district-/school-wide student achievement	1. Has district-/school-wide student achievement increased according to measures that are truly reflective of what students, ELs in particular, know and can do (in terms of learning of both language and content)? According to large-scale standardized tests?
	
	  a. If so, congratulations! What next steps are needed to ensure that this progress continues? (Move to analysis of each step in the ENGAGE model.)
	
	  b. If not, what are anticipated areas where improvement might have the biggest impact? (Move to analysis of each step of the ENGAGE model.)
		• Teacher-created assignment/ assessment scores
		  o with a focus on language development
		  o with a focus on content development
		• Differentiated grades
		• Teacher anecdotal records
		• Survey data (from administrators, teachers, and other stakeholders)
		• Large-scale standardized test scores
		• Evidence of communication about progress, success, and challenges

Establish a shared vision for serving ELs.	1. Does the vision statement in its current form accurately represent the goals of district/school?
	
	  a. If so, is it being enacted as planned?
	
	  b. If not, how does the vision need to be refined?
	
	2. What steps need to be taken to enhance the enactment of the vision?
		• The current vision statement
		• Anecdotal data collected by administrators, teachers, and stakeholders
		• Survey data (from administrators, teachers, and other stakeholders)

Name and capitalize upon relevant expertise within collaborative teams.	1. Has all relevant expertise at the district/school level been taken into account? (Are there newcomers to the district whose expertise has yet to be named and capitalized upon?) a. If not, what steps need to be taken to name and capitalize upon these untapped sources of expertise? 2. What steps must be taken to better capitalize upon district-/school-wide areas of expertise?	• Records of who was involved in this step in the process • Records of change in district/ school personnel • Anecdotal data collected by administrators, teachers, and stakeholders • Survey data (from administrators, teachers, and other stakeholders)

(Continued)

Table 7.1 (Continued)

Goal/Step in the ENGAGE Model	Guiding Questions	Potential Data Sources
Gather and analyze EL-specific data.	1. Have all relevant data been gathered and analyzed? That is, is the data gathering and analysis up to date? a. If so, are current data being used appropriately to guide assessment and instruction? b. If not, what steps need to be taken to gather and analyze these data and to ensure that they are used to guide assessment and instruction? 2. Have these data been shared with relevant school personnel?	• Previous data with analyses • Records of new students (to check that their data have been appropriately analyzed) • Records of data sharing with relevant personnel
Align standards-based assessments and grading with ELs' current levels of linguistic and content development.	1. Are assignments and assessments aligned with students' current levels of language and content development? a. If not, what steps need to be taken to ensure this alignment? 2. Is grading aligned with students' current levels of language and content development? a. If not, what steps need to be taken to ensure this alignment?	• Teacher-developed assignments and assessments • Teacher-developed differentiated scoring rubrics • Administrator monitoring data • Anecdotal data collected by administrators, teachers, and stakeholders • Survey data (from administrators, teachers, and other stakeholders)
Ground standards-based instruction in both content *and* language development	1. Is standards-based instruction grounded in content *and* language development? a. If not, what steps need to be taken to ensure this grounding?	• Records of curricular revision/redesign • Teacher lesson plans • Administrator monitoring data • Anecdotal data collected by administrators, teachers, and stakeholders • Survey data (from administrators, teachers, and other stakeholders)

The educator must believe in the potential power of his pupil, and he must employ all his art in seeking to bring his pupil to experience this power.

—Alfred Adler

RESOURCE 7.1 Template for Examining Results and Determining Next Steps

Goal/Step in the ENGAGE Model	Guiding Questions	Potential Data Sources	Next Steps	Persons Responsible	Timeline

Ultimate Goal: Increased district-/school-wide student achievement	1. Has district-/school-wide student achievement increased according to measures that are truly reflective of what students, ELs in particular, know and can do (in terms of learning of both language and content)? According to large-scale standardized tests?
	
	   a. If so, congratulations! What next steps are needed to ensure that this progress continues? (Move to analysis of each step in the ENGAGE model.)
	
	   b. If not, what are anticipated areas where improvement might have the biggest impact? (Move to analysis of each step of the ENGAGE model.)
		• Teacher-created assignment/assessment scores
		  ○ with a focus on language development
		  ○ with a focus on content development
		• Differentiated grades
		• Teacher anecdotal records
		• Survey data (from administrators, teachers, and other stakeholders)
		• Large-scale standardized test score			

Establish a shared vision for serving ELs.	1. Does the vision statement in its current form accurately represent the goals of district/school?
	
	   a. If so, is it being enacted as planned?
	
	   b. If not, how does the vision need to be refined?
	
	2. What steps need to be taken to enhance the enactment of the vision?
		• The current vision statement
		• Anecdotal data collected by administrators, teachers, and stakeholders
		• Survey data (from administrators, teachers, and other stakeholders)			

(Continued)

RESOURCE 7.1 (Continued)

Goal/Step in the ENGAGE Model	Guiding Questions	Potential Data Sources	Next Steps	Persons Responsible	Timeline
Name and capitalize upon relevant expertise within collaborative teams.	1. Has all relevant expertise at the district/ school level been taken into account? (Are there newcomers to the district whose expertise has yet to be named and capitalized upon?) a. If not, what steps need to be taken to name and capitalize upon these untapped sources of expertise? 2. What steps must be taken to better capitalize upon district–/school-wide areas of expertise?	• Records of who was involved in this step in the process • Records of change in district/school personnel • Anecdotal data collected by administrators, teachers, and stakeholders • Survey data (from administrators, teachers, and other stakeholders)			

Gather and analyze EL-specific data.	1. Have all relevant data been gathered and analyzed? That is, is the data gathering and analysis up-to-date?
	
	  a. If so, are current data being used appropriately to guide assessment and instruction?
	
	  b. If not, what steps need to be taken to gather and analyze these data and to ensure that they are used to guide assessment and instruction?
	
	2. Have these data been shared with relevant school personnel?
		• Previous data with analyses
		• Records of new students (to check that their data have been appropriately analyzed)
		• Records of data sharing with relevant personnel			

Goal/Step in the ENGAGE Model	Guiding Questions	Potential Data Sources	Next Steps	Persons Responsible	Timeline

Align standards-based assessments and grading with ELs' current levels of linguistic and content development	1. Are assignments and assessments aligned with students' current levels of language and content development?
	  a. If not, what steps need to be taken to ensure this alignment?
	2. Is grading aligned with students' current levels of language and content development?
	  a. If not, what steps need to be taken to ensure this alignment?
		• Teacher-developed assignments and assessments
		• Teacher-developed differentiated scoring rubrics
		• Administrator monitoring data
		• Anecdotal data collected by administrators, teachers, and stakeholders
		• Survey data (from administrators, teachers, and other stakeholders)			

Ground standards-based instruction in both content *and* language development	1. Is standards-based instruction grounded in content and language development? a. If not, what steps need to be taken to ensure this grounding?	• Records of curricular revision/redesign • Teacher lesson plans • Administrator monitoring data • Anecdotal data collected by administrators, teachers, and stakeholders • Survey data (from administrators, teachers, and other stakeholders)			

References

Abedi, J. (2009, December). *Assessment of English language learners.* Presentation at The Race to the Top Assessment Program Public & Expert Input Meeting, Denver, CO. Retrieved September 6, 2014, from http://www2.ed.gov/programs/racetothetop-assessment/bios/abedi-presentation.ppt

Alford, B. J., & Niño, M. C. (2011). *Leading academic achievement for English language learners: A guide for principals.* Thousand Oaks, CA: Corwin.

American Educational Research Association, American Psychological Association, & National Council on Measurement in Education. (1999). *Standards for education and psychological measurement.* Washington, DC: American Educational Research Association.

Bainbridge, S. (2007). *Creating a vision for your school.* London, UK: Paul Chapman Publishing.

Batalova, J., Fix, M., & Murray, J. (2007). *Measures of change: The demography and literacy of adolescent English learners.* Washington, DC: Migration Policy Institute.

Beck, I., McKeown, M. G., & Kucan, L. (2002). *Bringing words to life: Robust vocabulary instruction.* New York, NY: Guilford Press.

Bender, W. N., & Shore, C. (2007). *Response to intervention: A practical guide for every teacher.* Thousand Oaks, CA: Corwin.

Butler, F. A., & Stevens, R. (1997). *Accommodation strategies for English language learners on large-scale assessments: Student characteristics and other considerations* (Technical Report No. 448). Los Angeles, CA: National Center for Research on Evaluation, Standards, and Student Testing (CRESST). Available at http://www.cresst.org

Calderón, M., Slavin, R., & Sánchez, M. (2011). Effective instruction for English learners. *The Future of Children, 21*(1), 103–127.

Callahan, R. M. (2013, February). *The English learner dropout dilemma: Multiple risks and multiple resources.* Policy Brief 19. California Dropout Research Project. Available at http://www.cdrp.ucsb.edu/pubs_reports.htm

Castellano, J. A., & Diaz, E. I. (2002). *Reaching new horizons: Gifted and talented education for culturally and linguistically diverse students.* Boston, MA: Allyn & Bacon.

Chamberlain, S. P., Guerra, P., & Garcia, S. B. (1999). *Intercultural communication in the classroom.* (ERIC ED 432573). Retrieved August 30, 2014, from http://files.eric.ed.gov/fulltext/ED432573.pdf

Coleman, R., & Goldenberg, C. (2012). The Common Core challenge for ELLs. *Principal Leadership*, pp. 46–51. Retrieved April 7, 2015, from https://csmp .ucop.edu/resources/materials/pl_feb12_goldenberg.pdf

Collier, V. P., & Thomas, W. P. (2009). *Educating English learners for a transformed world.* Albuquerque, NM: Fuente Press.

Cummins, J. (2001). Linguistic interdependence and the educational development of bilingual children. In C. Baker & N. H. Hornberger (Eds.), *An introductory reader to the writings of Jim Cummins* (pp. 63–95.). Buffalo, NY: Multilingual Matters.

Custodio, B. (2011). *How to design and implement a newcomer program.* Boston, MA: Pearson.

Early Head Start Resource Center @ ZERO TO THREE. (n.d.). *Revisiting and updating the multicultural principles for Head Start programs serving children ages birth to five: Addressing culture and home language in Head Start Program systems & services.* Retrieved March 1, 2014, from https://eclkc.ohs.acf.hhs.gov/hslc/ hs/resources/ECLKC_Bookstore/PDFs/Revisiting%20Multicultural%20 Principles%20for%20Head%20Start_English.pdf

Echevarria, J., Vogt, M., & Short, D. (2013). *Making content comprehensible for English learners: The SIOP model* (4th ed.). Boston, MA: Pearson Education.

EdSource. (2007, September). *Similar English learner students, different results: Why do some schools do better?* Retrieved November 13, 2014, from http:// files.eric.ed.gov/fulltext/ED500473.pdf

Fairbairn, S., & Fox, J. (2009). Inclusive achievement testing for linguistically and culturally diverse test takers: Essential considerations for test developers and decision makers. *Educational Measurement: Issues and Practice, 28*(1), 10–24.

Fairbairn, S., & Jones-Vo, S. (2010). *Differentiating instruction and assessment for English language learners: A guide for K–12 Teachers.* Philadelphia, PA: Caslon.

Fan, X., & Chen, M. (2001). Involvement and students' academic achievement: A meta-analysis. *Educational Psychology Review, 13*(1), 1–22.

Freeman, D. E., & Freeman, Y. S. (2004). *Essential linguistics: What you need to know to teach reading, ESL, spelling, phonics, and grammar.* Portsmouth, NH: Heinemann.

Fry, R. (2007, April). *How far behind in reading and math are English language learners?* Washington, DC: Hew Hispanic Center. Retrieved February 16, 2014, from http://files.eric.ed.gov/fulltext/ED509863.pdf

Fullan, M. (2011a). *Choosing the wrong drivers for whole system reform.* Seminar Series 204. Melbourne, Australia: Centre for Strategic Education. Retrieved January 25, 2014, from http://iowaascd.org/files/6913/3305/3467/ Fullan_Wrong_Drivers.pdf

Fullan, M. (2011b). *Learning is the work* (Unpublished manuscript). Education in Motion. Retrieved January 25, 2014, from http://iowaascd.org/files/ 1613/2450/7568/11_July_Fullan_Learning_is_the_Work.pdf

Galguera, T. (2011). Participant structures as professional learning tasks and the development of pedagogical language knowledge among preservice teachers. *Teacher Education Quarterly,* Winter, 85–106. Retrieved April 1, 2015, from http://files.eric.ed.gov/fulltext/EJ914925.pdf

Garmston, R. J., & Wellman, B. M. (2013). *The adaptive school: A sourcebook for developing collaborative groups* (2nd ed.). Lanham, MD: Rowman & Littlefield.

Genessee, F., & Riches, C. (2006). Literacy: Instructional issues. In F. Genessee, K. Lindholm-Leary, W. M. Saunders, & D. Christian (Eds.), *Educating English language learners: A synthesis of research evidence* (pp. 109–175). New York, NY: Cambridge University Press.

Ghiso, M. P. (2012). How do we ensure that English language learners can read and write in all content areas? In E. Hamayan & R. Freeman Field (Eds.), *English language learners at school: A guide for administrators* (pp. 183–186). Philadelphia, PA: Caslon.

Goldenberg, C. (2008). Teaching English language learners: What the research does—and does not—say. *American Educator, 32*(2), 8–23, 43–44. Retrieved November 13, 2014, from https://www.aft.org//sites/default/files/periodicals/goldenberg.pdf

Gordon, J., & Morales, L. (2012). What materials can we use with English language learners? In R. Freeman-Field & E. Hamayan (Eds.), *English language learners in school: A guide for administrators* (2nd ed.) (pp. 186–188). Philadelphia, PA: Caslon.

Grey, M., & Devlin, M. (n.d.). *Rapid ethnic diversification and microplurality: Implications of Iowa's new demographics for communities.* Retrieved February 16, 2014, from https://www.dordt.edu/services_support/andreas_center/past_projects/immigration/devlin_and_grey.ppt

Guskey, T. R., & Bailey, J. M. (2010). *Developing standards-based report cards.* Thousand Oaks, CA: Corwin.

Hakuta, K., Butler, Y. G., & Witt, D. (2000). *How long does it take English learners to attain proficiency?* (Policy Report 2000–1). California: The University of California Linguistic Minority Research Institute. Retrieved March 8, 2014, from http://www.stanford.edu/~hakuta/Publications/(2000)%20-%20HOW%20LONG%20DOES%20IT%20TAKE%20ENGLISH%20LEARNERS%20TO%20ATTAIN%20PR.pdf

Hamayan, E., Marler, B., Sanchez-Lopez, C., & Damico, J. (2013). *Special education considerations for English language learners: Delivering a continuum of services* (2nd ed.). Philadelphia, PA: Caslon.

Haynes, M. (2012). *The role of language and literacy in college- and career-reading standards: Rethinking policy and practice in support of English language learners.* Washington, DC: Alliance for Excellent Education. Retrieved January, 25, 2014, from a114ed.org/wp-content/uploads/2013/06/LangAndLiteracyInStandardsELLs.pdf

Hess, K. (2011). *Learning progressions frameworks designed for use with the Common Core State Standards in English language arts & literacy K–12.* Retrieved October 19, 2014, from http://www.naacpartners.org/publications/ela_lpf_12.2011_final.pdf

Honigsfeld, A., & Dove, M. G. (2010). *Collaboration and co-teaching: Strategies for English learners.* Thousand Oaks, CA: Corwin.

Jones-Vo, S., & Fairbairn, S. (2012, August 31). Positioning ELLs at the core of the Core: A model for engagement and achievement. *The Source.* Invited online article archived at http://archive.constantcontact.com/fs084/11040152 96037/archive/1110732002537.html

Jones-Vo, S., Fairbairn, S., Hiatt, J., Simmons, M., Looker, J., & Kinley, J. (2007). Increasing ELL achievement through reciprocal mentoring. *Journal of Content Area Reading, 6*(1), 21–44.

Jung, L. A., & Guskey, T. R. (2010). Grading exceptional learners. *Educational Leadership, 67*(5), 31–35.

Jung, L. A., & Guskey, T. R. (2012). *Grading exceptional and struggling learners.* Thousand Oaks, CA: Corwin.

Kinsella, K., & Singer, T. W. (2011). *Linguistic scaffolds for writing effective language objectives.* Retrieved November 4, 2014, from https://www.scoe.org/files/kinsella-handouts.pdf

Knight, J. (2007). *Instructional coaching: A partnership approach to improving instruction.* Thousand Oaks, CA: Corwin.

Kopriva, R. (2000). *Ensuring accuracy in testing for English language learners.* Washington, DC: Council of Chief State School Officers.

Kopriva, R. J., Emick, J. E., Hipolito-Delgado, C. P., & Cameron, C. A. (2007). Do proper accommodation assignments make a difference? Examining the impact of improved decision making on scores for English language learners. *Educational Measurement: Issues and Practice, 26*(3), 11–20.

Linan-Thompson, S., Cirino, P. T., & Vaughn, S. (2007). Determining English language learners' response to intervention: Questions and some answers. *Learning Disability Quarterly, 30,* 185–195.

Linan-Thompson, S., & Vaughn, S. (2007). *Research-based methods of reading instruction for English language learners, Grades K–4.* Alexandria, VA: ASCD.

Linton, C., & Davis, B. (2013). *Equity 101: Culture—Book 2.* Thousand Oaks, CA: Corwin.

Marzano, R. J. (2010). *Formative assessment & standards-based grading: Classroom strategies that work.* Bloomington, IN: Marzano Research Laboratory.

Mather, M. (2009). *Reports on America: Children in immigrant families chart new path.* Washington, DC: Population Reference Bureau. Retrieved August 11, 2012, from http://www.prb.org/pdf09/immigrantchildren.pdf

Maxwell, L. A. (2012, August). Mass. moves on ELL-training for regular teachers. *Education Week.* Retrieved February 14, 2014, from http://www.edweek.org/ew/articles/2012/08/08/37massell.h31.html

Mellard, D. F., & Johnson, E. S. (2008). *RTI: A practitioner's guide to implementing response to intervention.* Thousand Oaks, CA: Corwin.

Menken, K. (2000). *What are the critical issues in wide-scale assessment of English language learners?* Issue Brief No. 6. Washington, DC: National Clearinghouse for Bilingual Education. Retrieved September 30, 2006, from http://www.ncela.gwu.edu/pubs/issuebriefs/ib6.htm

Moll, L. (1992). Bilingual classroom studies and community analysis: Some recent trends. *Educational Researcher, 21*(2), 20–24.

National Clearinghouse for English Language Acquisition (NCELA). (2011a). *The growing numbers of English language learners, 2009/10.* Retrieved February 7, 2014, from http://www.ncela.us/files/uploads/9/growing_EL_0910.pdf

National Clearinghouse for English Language Acquisition (NCELA). (2011b). *What languages do English learners speak?* NCELA Fact Sheet. Washington, DC: Author. Available from http://www.ncela.us/files/uploads/NCELAFactsheets/EL_Languages_2011.pdf

Next Generation Science Standards. (2013). *APPENDIX E—Progressions within the Next Generation Science Standards.* Retrieved October 19, 2014, from http://www.nextgenscience.org/sites/ngss/files/Appendix%20E%20-%20Progressions%20within%20NGSS%20-%20052213.pdf

Nguyen, D. (2013, June). *Implementing RtI with ELLs: Challenges and promises.* Workshop presented at the Our Kids Summer Institute, Waukee, IA.

O'Connor, K. (2009). *How to grade for learning K–12* (3rd ed.). Thousand Oaks, CA: Corwin.

Olsen, L. (2010). *Reparable harm: Fulfilling the unkept promise of educational opportunity for California's long-term English learners.* Long Beach, CA: Californians Together. Retrieved February 11, 2015, from http://californianstogether.org

Omaggio, A. C. (1979). Pictures and second language comprehension: Do they help? *Foreign Language Annals, 12*(2), 107–116.

Peters, R. & Buckmiller, T. (2014). Our grades were broken: Overcoming barriers and challenges to implementing standards-based grading. *Journal of Educational Leadership in Action, 2*(2). Retrieved April 8, 2015, from http://www.lindenwood.edu/ela/issue04/buckmiller.html

Popham, W. J. (2014). Criterion-referenced measurement? Half a century wasted? *Educational Leadership, 71*(6), 62–67.

Quirk, M., & Beem, S. (2012). Examining the relations between reading fluency and reading comprehension for English language learners. *Psychology in the Schools, 49*(6), 539–553.

Ross, T. (2014). Welcome: Crescent Town Elementary School Visit. Celebrating Linguistic Diversity Conference Pre-Conference School Tour, Toronto, Canada, April 29, 2014.

Rothstein-Fisch, C., & Trumbull, E. (2008). *Managing diverse classrooms: How to build on students' cultural strengths.* Alexandria, VA: ASCD.

Samson, J. F., & Collins, B. A. (2012, April). *Preparing all teachers to meet the needs of English language learners: Applying research policy and practice for teacher effectiveness.* Washington, DC: Center for American Progress. Retrieved February 16, 2014, from http://www.americanprogress.org/wp-content/uploads/issues/2012/04/pdf/ell_report.pdf

Senge, P., Cambron-McCabe, N., Lucas, T., Smith, B., Dutton, J., & Kleiner, A. (2012). *Schools that learn: A fifth discipline fieldbook for educators, parents, and everyone who cares about education.* New York, NY: Crown Business.

Settlement Agreement Between the United States of America and the Boston Public Schools. (n.d.). Retrieved February 14, 2014, from http://www.edweek.org/media/09–30–10_final_agreement%5B1%5D.pdf

Shin, H. B., & Kominski, R. A. (2010, April). *Language use in the United States: 2007.* American Community Survey Reports, ACS-12. Washington, DC: US Census Bureau. Retrieved February 16, 2014, from http://www.census.gov/hhes/socdemo/language/data/acs/ACS-12.pdf

Short, D. J., & Fitzsimmons, S. (2007). *Double the work: Challenges and solutions to acquiring language and academic literacy for adolescent English language learners.* New York, NY: Carnegie Corporation. Retrieved March 1, 2014, from http://carnegie.org/fileadmin/Media/Publications/PDF/DoubletheWork.pdf

Snow, C., Burns, M. S., & Griffin, P. (Eds.). (1998). *Preventing reading difficulties in young children.* Washington, DC: National Academy Press.

Solano-Flores, G., Trumbull, E., & Nelson-Barber, S. (2002). Concurrent development of dual language assessments: An alternative to translating tests for linguistic minorities. *International Journal of Testing, 2*(2), 107–129.

Staehr Fenner, D. (2013, January). *Preparing all teachers of ELLs for the CCSS.* Colorín Colorado. Retrieved February 16, 2014, from http://blog.colorincolorado.org/2013/01/28/teacher-preparation-of-ells-for-the-ccss/

Stevens, R. A., Butler, F. A., & Castellon-Wellington, M. (2000). Academic language and content assessment: *Measuring the progress of English language learners (ELLs).* (Research Report No. 552). Los Angeles, CA: National Center for Research on Evaluation, Standards, and Student Testing (CRESST). Retrieved September 6, 2014, from http://www.cse.ucla.edu/products/reports/TR552.pdf

Teachers of English to Speakers of Other Languages (TESOL), Inc. (2006a). *PreK–12 English language proficiency standards.* Alexandria, VA: Author.

Teachers of English to Speakers of Other Languages (TESOL), Inc. (2006b). TESOL *PreK–12 English Language Proficiency Standards Framework.* Retrieved November 1, 2014, from http://www.tesol.org/docs/books/bk_prek-12elpstandards_framework_318.pdf

Teachers of English to Speakers of Other Languages (TESOL), Inc. (2009). *Paper to practice: Using the TESOL English language proficiency standards in PreK–12 classrooms.* Alexandria, VA: Author.

Ting-Toomey, S., & Chung, L. C. (2005). *Understanding intercultural communication.* New York, NY: Oxford University Press.

Ting-Toomey, S., & Chung, L. C. (2011). *Understanding intercultural communication* (2nd ed.). New York, NY: Oxford University Press.

Tomlinson, C. A. (2005). *How to differentiate instruction in mixed-ability classrooms* (2nd ed.). Upper Saddle River, NJ: Pearson Merrill Prentice Hall.

United Nations High Commissioner for Refugees (UNHCR). (2007). *The 1951 refugee convention: Questions and answers.* Geneva, Switzerland: Author. Retrieved February 9, 2009, from http://www.unhcr.org/basics/BASICS/3c0f495f4.pdf

US Department of Education, Office of Planning, Evaluation and Policy Development, Policy and Program Studies Service. (2012). *National Evaluation of Title III implementation—Report on state and local implementa-*

tion. Retrieved August 11, 2012, from http://www.air.org/files/AIR_Title_III_Implementation.pdf

US Department of Justice & US Department of Education. (2015). *Ensuring English learner students can participate meaningfully and equally in educational programs.* Retrieved February 15, 2015, from http://www2.ed.gov/about/offices/list/ocr/docs/dcl-factsheet-el-students-201501.pdf

Wagner, T., Kegan, R., Lahey, L., Lemons, R. W., Garnier, J., Helsing, D. Howell, A., & Rassmussen, H. T. (2006). *Change leadership: A practical guide to transforming our schools.* San Francisco, CA: Jossey-Bass.

Walker, C. L., & Stone, K. (2011). Preparing teachers to reach English language learners. In T. Lucas (Ed.), *Teacher preparation for linguistically diverse classrooms: A resource for teacher educators* (pp. 127–142). New York, NY: Taylor and Francis.

WIDA. (n.d.a). *PreK—grade 12 can do descriptors.* Available at http://www.wida.us/standards/CAN_DOs/

WIDA. (n.d.b). *WIDA performance definitions: Listening and speaking, K–12.* Retrieved November 8, 2014, from http://www.wida.us/DownloadDocs/standards/2012Amplification/WIDA_Performance%20Definitions_ListeningReading.pdf

WIDA. (n.d.c). *WIDA performance definitions: Speaking and writing, K–12.* Retrieved November 8, 2014, from http://www.wida.us/DownloadDocs/standards/2012Amplification/WIDA_Performance%20Definitions_SpeakingWriting.pdf

Wiggins, G., & McTighe, J. (2006). *Understanding by design* (2nd ed.). Boston, MA: Pearson.

Wong-Fillmore, L. (2000). Loss of family languages: Should educators be concerned? *Theory Into Practice, 39*(4), 203–210.

Wormeli, R. (2006). *Fair isn't always equal: Assessing and grading in the differentiated classroom.* Portsmouth, NH: Stenhouse.

Index

A SAGE Company

Helping educators make the greatest impact

CORWIN HAS ONE MISSION: to enhance education through intentional professional learning.

We build long-term relationships with our authors, educators, clients, and associations who partner with us to develop and continuously improve the best evidence-based practices that establish and support lifelong learning.